INVESTING
IN THE SECOND
LOST DECADE

INVESTING IN THE SECOND LOST DECADE

A SURVIVAL GUIDE FOR KEEPING YOUR PROFITS UP WHEN THE MARKET IS DOWN

MARTIN J. PRING

JOE D. TURNER • TOM J. KOPAS

NEW YORK CHICAGO SAN FRANCISCO
LISBON LONDON MADRID MEXICO CITY MILAN
NEW DELHI SAN JUAN SEOUL SINGAPORE
SYDNEY TORONTO

The McGraw·Hill Companies

1 2 3 4 5 6 7 8 9 0   DOC/DOC   1 8 7 6 5 4 3 2

ISBN   978-0-07-179744-3
MHID   0-07-179744-0

e-ISBN 978-0-07-179745-0
e-MHID   0-07-179745-9

This publication is designed to provide accurate and authoritative information in regard to the subject matter covered. It is sold with the understanding that neither the author nor the publisher is engaged in rendering legal, accounting, securities trading, or other professional services. If legal advice or other expert assistance is required, the services of a competent professional person should be sought.

> —From a Declaration of Principles Jointly Adopted by a Committee of the American Bar Association and a Committee of Publishers and Associations

Library of Congress Cataloging-in-Publication Data

Pring, Martin J.
    Investing in the second lost decade : a survival guide for keeping your profits up when the market is down / by Martin J. Pring and Joe D. Turner and Tom J. Kopas. — 1st ed.
      p.   cm.
    Includes index.
    ISBN 978-0-07-179744-3 (alk. paper) — ISBN 0-07-179744-0 (alk. paper)
    1. Investments.   2. Portfolio management. I. Turner, Joe D. II. Kopas, Tom J. III. Title.
    HG4521.P8355   2012
    332.6—dc23

                       2012009343

McGraw-Hill books are available at special quantity discounts to use as premiums and sales promotions or for use in corporate training programs. To contact a representative, please e-mail us at bulksales@mcgraw-hill.com.

This book is printed on acid-free paper.

This book is dedicated to the very important people in our lives:

- Nancy King—a key person at the center of Pring Turner Capital Group who reliably and diligently makes sure our office runs smoothly. She has been for many years a steadfast rock for us and our clients.
- Our clients—thank you for your patience and entrusting us with the responsibility to guard and grow your valuable assets.
- Our families—especially our wives Lisa Pring, Tina Turner, and Lili Kopas who provide the much needed support and encouragement in our pursuit of helping others reach financial peace of mind. Our children, who are always on our minds, inspire us to reach higher standards and levels of achievement.

Jason Pring
Laura Pring Lincoln
Constance Pring
Thomas Pring

Theron Turner
Shad Turner
Tiffanny Turner Brooks

Jim Kopas
Will Kopas
Alli Kopas

CONTENTS

ACKNOWLEDGMENTS

No book can be written without help and inspiration from a number of valuable contributors to the project. We are especially thankful for the intellectual impact of the educational community, which includes Dr. Henry "Hank" Pruden, professor at Golden Gate University in San Francisco. Hank, a longtime educator and advocate of market analysis, was the original matchmaker who introduced Martin Pring to Joe Turner. This eventually led to the formation of Pring Turner Capital Group in 1988. Another long-term associate, friend, advisor, and innovative educator is Bruce Fraser, to whom we are indebted for pushing all of us further and higher in pursuit of portfolio management mastery. Additionally, we give special thanks to Robin Parker who also opened our minds to reach a greater understanding of our own unique offering to the investment world.

We acknowledge the good people at Dow Jones Indexes who discovered Martin Pring's business cycle research and validated the long-standing investment approach of Pring Turner Capital Group that is detailed and utilized in this book. Certain chapters in this book would not be possible without the exhaustive research efforts conducted by Steven Malinsky, David Krein, and Jeff Fernandez. The team at Dow Jones Indexes was instrumental in developing the Dow Jones Pring U.S. Business Cycle Index.

A special thank you to Richard Ciuba at Dow Jones Indexes for introducing us to Noah Hamman at AdvisorShares who had the idea to launch an actively managed exchange-traded fund based on our business cycle strategy. We are looking forward, by early 2013, to introducing the Pring Turner Dow Jones Business Cycle ETF (symbol DBIZ) to advisors and investors who have been searching for an "all-seasons" investment vehicle.

We appreciate the efforts of the staff at McGraw-Hill, especially Mary Glenn and Jane Palmieri for their patience and for tolerating all our editorial shortcomings. They worked with our raw material, pushed us on deadlines, and took the book past the finish line.

INTRODUCTION

ARE YOU PREPARED FOR *ANOTHER* LOST DECADE AHEAD?

Ahh, the good old days. Remember when investing was fun and easy in the 1990s as investors enjoyed the late stages of a raging bull market? From 1995 to 1999 the S&P 500 posted consecutive annual returns of 38 percent, 23 percent, 33 percent, 29 percent, and 21 percent, respectively. To put that into perspective, a $1 million investment on January 1, 1995, grew to nearly $3.5 million by the turn of the century, and those returns appear tame in comparison to the astronomical fortunes made in the technology-laden Nasdaq index (an 85 percent return in 1999 alone). Ten-, fifteen-, and twenty-year stock market returns sported hefty midteen average annual returns. Back then, investment decisions were fairly easy to make. All an investor had to do was buy a ticket and stay onboard the runaway stock market train heading higher. The undeniable investment mantra drilled into all participants was simply: buy the dips, buy and hold, and sit back and watch your profits multiply. Spectacular stock market gains built over the prior 18 years reinforced a "can't lose" mentality. Everyone was an investment genius and bragged about it at any opportunity whether it was on the golf course, around the office water cooler, or even during the family Thanksgiving dinner. Day trading replaced many a career—it was more fun and paid better than, say, that boring professional career with the less than adequate attorneys' salary. Even the most conservative of investors got caught up in the greed contagion, left their risk-averse tendencies behind, and joined the party. Then something happened. As the world entered the new millennium and the year 2000 struck, the investment climate changed dramatically. Something investors had not dealt with since the late 1960s began—a long-term or "secular" bear market emerged. All of a sudden the well-ingrained rules of the investment world changed completely, and portfolio decision making became far more difficult.

More than 10 years later, many investors and members of the financial press recognized that stock prices actually lost ground, labeling this period the "lost decade." Indeed, the period from January 2000 through December 2009 goes down in history as one of the worst 10-year investment periods ever for stocks. Two severe 50 percent-plus bear markets over the decade demoralized buy-and-hold investors, leading to a −9 percent loss including dividends. A new cold reality set in. Expectations of annual double-digit stock market returns no longer dance in investors' minds. Stories of individuals leaving their jobs to day-trade are long past—in 2012, people are satisfied just to have a full-time job. Other once dependable investment alternatives have their own legitimate concerns. The myth that real estate is a low-risk investment and only goes up has been thoroughly shattered. Earnings on savings accounts have plummeted to near zero, and after the effects of inflation and taxes are actually negative. Government bond yields are at generational lows and offer little return potential and substantial principal risk if interest rates should go up. Yes, since 2000 investing has been a veritable minefield for most investors. A decade that began with wild-eyed optimism and confidence ended with investors anxious with fear and holding sobered expectations.

To illustrate our point, let's take a close look at one couple's retirement plans and how expectations changed since 2000. Mr. Smith was age 62 when he and Mrs. Smith decided to retire with a sizable nest egg. Using history as a guide, they decide to allocate $1 million of retirement savings to the stock market via a passive index fund. After all, at that time the S&P 500 had delivered 25-year average annual returns of over 17 percent, and since 1900 the performance averaged about 10 percent per year. They figured if they could earn just 10 percent and spend half the earnings, they would be able to leave the remaining 5 percent of earnings to compound. This seemingly sensible strategy would allow their retirement nest egg to continue to grow and even provide a "pay raise" from time to time to offset inflation. They planned to withdraw $50,000 annually ($12,500 quarterly) to help fund their living expenses. This sounded reasonable at the time—the Smiths weren't being too greedy. At least they thought they made realistic assumptions and had reasonable expectations. After a dozen years in retirement (as 2012 began), Mr. Smith was a 74-year-old retiree, and Chart I-1 shows what happened to the $1 million nest egg.

Combined with a "lost decade" of negative total stock market returns and a steady withdrawal rate, they end the first 12 years of retirement with a portfolio balance of only $330,225. How much longer will they be able to tap that portfolio for living expenses? And what will the Smiths do if, as we suspect and elaborate on in this book, there is *another* lost decade ahead? When will they run out of money? We will continue to check in with the Smiths throughout this book to better illustrate the financial landscape and offer proactive solutions to help people adapt to the difficult task of surviving and prospering in *another* lost decade we believe lies ahead.

While it is true that in the very long run stocks go up, it is also true that secular bear markets are a fact of life. These dangerous very long-term time periods where stocks underperform can last 20 years or

CHART I-1 Will the Smiths Outlive Their Retirement Nest Egg?
The combination of the "lost decade" for stocks and steady withdrawals for
retirement income leaves the Smiths' nest egg severely depleted. How will they
survive a *second* lost decade?

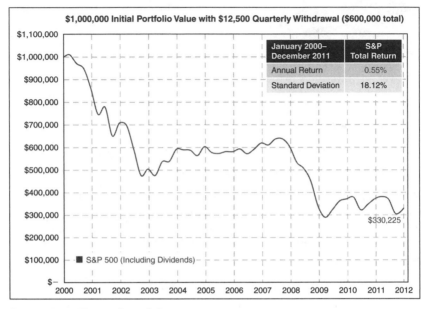

Source: Pring Turner Capital Group

more. How many of these 20-year periods do you have in your investment lifetime? Can Mr. and Mrs. Smith afford to stick it out with a
passive buy-and-hold index approach through another lost decade?
By the end of that decade, they will be in their early eighties and eager
for the next secular bull market to begin. The question is: Will they
have any money left by then? Our point is that in order to be successful, it is vitally important for investors to understand what secular
environment they are in. Is it a secular bull market or secular bear
market? We know the secular bull markets (like the one from 1982 to
2000) are pretty easy to navigate—simply buy and hold. But, secular
bear markets are a different animal altogether with many cyclical ups
and downs. Succeeding in a secular bear market takes a lot of hard
work, the right tools, and a more flexible investment discipline. Our

goal is to thoroughly demonstrate these disciplines so you can successfully maneuver through the remainder of the next lost decade.

The good news is that it is possible to build wealth during a secular bear market, but investors must first discard the buy-and-hold, indexing, and passive asset allocation strategies that worked well in the prior secular bull market. In a negative secular bear market environment the same static methods result in severely inadequate returns. The crucial determinant to building wealth successfully in a secular bear market is to adopt a more *proactive* plan of action. Even in this difficult, uphill, overall negative atmosphere there will be rewarding opportunities—these are the cyclical upturns that may last two or three years. And these will be followed by cyclical declines where careful risk-management techniques must be employed to protect portfolio values and preserve the hard-earned gains of the prior advance. The key to the successful exploitation of these moves is the application of the proper business cycle forecasting tools and disciplines. The last 150 years of economic and financial history show that markets are linked in a logical way to business activity. The economy goes through a set series of chronological sequences just like the seasons of the year.

Recognizing these "financial seasons" and correctly applying the appropriate asset allocation have always had a beneficial impact on investment returns. Indeed, investors can benefit from understanding the historical, reliable, and sequential relationship of the business cycle to stocks, bonds, and inflation-sensitive assets. With knowledge of business cycles, secular trends, and timely tactical asset allocation, it is possible to create better returns with less risk and, most important, to experience peace of mind.

Some people say it is probably a good idea to learn a little about the author before reading a book. That way the reader can better understand the authors' biases and point of view. This book is coauthored by the partners at Pring Turner Capital Group—Martin Pring,

Joe Turner, and Tom Kopas combine for over 110 years of experience in the financial markets. We also would like to credit associate portfolio manager Jim Kopas for his thorough research work, editing, and digital production efforts, which were invaluable contributions to this project.

For decades, our conservative money management firm has successfully utilized the key elements of the strategies detailed in the pages ahead. Our approach is unique in that it is multifaceted and includes elements of fundamental, technical, and business cycle analysis. The reason we take this wide-ranging view of portfolio management is that our first and overriding goal is careful risk management. In fact, in our office the "cosmic joke" we govern ourselves by is: "We don't know." We don't know specifically what the future will bring. Nobody does. Yet we have to make decisions today, with an unknown future, and come out the other end with a successful outcome for clients. This is why we rely on the repetitive nature of the business cycle and pay a lot of attention to risk management.

Certainly, there are elements of fundamental analysis (quality, value, income), technical analysis (trend analysis, investor sentiment, and monetary policy), and business cycle analysis (economic turning points) that can help smooth out the ride for investors. We see all these elements as layers of risk management for portfolios because we do not exactly know what the future brings. However, with the right combination of tools, it is possible to reduce risk and improve returns.

In terms of our style, we are not day traders, certainly not high-frequency traders, but we are not "buy and hold" types either. Our asset allocations are not passive as is the case with most financial advisors; instead we use a dynamic approach that is determined to a large extent by where we are in the typical four- to five-year business cycle. Allocation changes and sector emphasis around the cycle are made gradually and methodically. As the evidence changes, we change. The important distinction is that our allocation decisions are based on looking at the markets and the economy to determine risk and reward trade-offs for the various asset classes. Conventional wisdom says that you can use age as a determinant for portfolio allocation, with the idea that at age 35 you can take more risk because you have more time to make back the loss. Our view is that regardless of whether you are 35, 55, or 75 years old, you simply do not want too much exposure to stocks going into a bear market–led recession. Being younger and having plenty of time to make money back doesn't justify losing it in the first place. Secular (very long term) and business cycle–associated bull and bear markets do not discriminate based on age.

We spent time looking back at history to learn from prior secular bear markets. These lessons will help you prepare for what lies ahead. And just what does lie ahead? Our opinion, based on extensive studies of previous secular bear markets, strongly suggests that investors should anticipate and prepare for *another* "lost decade" for stocks. Expect a decade with more frequent recessions and shorter and less robust recoveries. In fact, we believe that the next 10 years will be even more difficult than the last 10 because of a new emerging menace— inflation! It may not happen right away because of the deflationary difficulties associated with the debt overhang, discussed at great length in Chapter 3. However, we feel that government policy is heading in the direction of monetizing the sizable debt load—the easiest way for politicians to offset the debt buildup is to inflate, or simply print more money. After World War I, during the Weimar Republic in Germany, it took several years of aggressive money printing before prices took off to the extent that the paper currency essentially became worthless. We are certainly not forecasting such extreme conditions, but it is important to note that inflation is a stealth tax that penalizes savers and can wreak havoc on retiree lifestyles. It is an enemy investors have not had to really face since the 1970s and early 1980s. We are on alert.

How prepared are you to meet this new challenge? What if you not only have to deal with a secular bear market for stocks but also a new secular bear market for bonds? If inflation and interest rates rise over the next 10 years, bonds may be just as miserable an investment as stocks have been during the last decade. What if both of those markets face a challenging, deeply cyclical environment? How can you fully prepare? Will you be a victim of market forces or empowered to control your investment destiny?

By the time you get to the end of this book, you will have the critical tools and tactics you need to handle whatever comes your way in another lost decade. We explain how it's possible to execute two game plans: one designed to protect assets in the cyclical bear markets and another to grow wealth in the cyclical upturns. A constant theme incorporates critical risk-management tools to first protect and then grow wealth throughout both good and bad cycles. For those seeking an even deeper understanding of the material, we provide detailed appendixes that expand on the key topics. Moreover, www.pringturner.com will periodically bring you up to date on our current thinking as well as on the latest charts. Also, a wealth of resources including a reproduction of all the charts and figures in color, useful links, and a video of our business cycle approach to investing can be found at www.mhprofessional.com/mediacenter/. Whether you are a financial professional or individual investor, this book is designed to be an invaluable, practical guide to help you not only survive but also prosper in the second lost decade.

INVESTING
IN THE SECOND
LOST DECADE

CHAPTER 1

WHY A SECOND LOST DECADE LIES AHEAD

The year 1553 saw Lady Jane Grey deposed from the throne of England after only nine days in the palace. This event has absolutely nothing to do with the subject of surviving the second lost decade, except for one thing. The number 1,553 marks the secular bull market peak in the S&P 500 composite on March 24, 2000. Prior to that date U.S. equities experienced an 18-year secular or very long-term bull market. Since then stock prices have been in a bear market, often labeled as the "lost decade" for investors. Nothing unusual happened on that early spring day in 2000, no one rang a bell to herald the passing of the bull, and no one realized that a new, more challenging investment era had begun. No broker called Mr. Smith to tell him the bad news. As usual the market transitioned quietly to a secular bear market without any fanfare announcing the painful shift awaiting complacent investors.

Two Types of Economic Turning Points

The economic history of the United States is littered with turning points initiated by financial panics, crashes, and banking failures followed by depressions or recessions. Not all turning points are created equal though, because it is possible to break turning points down into two broad categories as their repercussions are substantially different. The first is a normal business cycle peak marking the top of a typical recovery. Let us call that a *cyclical* turning point. The downturn that follows can be triggered by many factors, such as excessive inventories requiring liquidation and "unexpected" rises in interest rates that catch investors unaware. The principal characteristic of this cyclical type of reversal is that the problem can be corrected relatively easily once a brief period of pain and adjustment is made—a garden variety recession.

The second type of turning point is akin to the one that began on March 24, 2000—a more serious affair because it is structural in nature. Much like the difference between catching a cold and having open heart surgery. A cold is unpleasant to experience, but it soon passes and leaves no physical traces. On the other hand, open heart surgery results in a traumatic shock to the body and takes much longer for a full recovery. Eventually surgery leaves no permanent damage except for the scar caused by the surgeon's scalpel. These less frequent very long-term turning points are known as *secular* reversals. Just like a patient, the economy eventually recovers from one of these long-term declines, but it takes many years, even decades, and several business cycles to do so. This chapter describes some of the economic and financial forces causing these tectonic shifts and explains why we believe *another* lost decade lies ahead.

A run-of-the-mill business cycle recession is normally triggered by inventory adjustments. Corporations extrapolate recent sales growth trends and build up inventories anticipating further growth during the latter frantic part of an expansion. Then as sales unexpectedly begin to drop, there is a period when companies cannot liquidate inventories fast enough, and cash flow turns negative. For a temporary period they are forced to go to the bank and finance the difference. Since the demand for credit increases, its price, namely interest rates, goes up. This in turn causes overall demand in the economy to tumble. Finally, excess inventories are liquidated, recently acquired loans are paid off, and the economy is ready for the next recovery. This is a fairly simplistic explanation because in the real world there are different reasons for individual recessions. The main point to bear in mind is that during a normal business cycle recession the pain is relatively short-lived as the excesses of the prior expansion are worked off.

Secular turning points like the one that took place in March 2000 develop when financial excesses are allowed to grow, creating huge economic distortions over the course of many business cycles and finally coming to a tipping point. A common theme in the vast majority of these situations is the massive buildup of excessive debt. When a structural problem develops, it is far more difficult to work through than a typical inventory recession. Two great examples of secular excesses are canal and railroad expansion in the early and mid part of the nineteenth century, respectively. Both innovations in transportation began as sensible projects, where a respectable rate of return on capital was expected over a reasonable time. The problem developed over the course of several business cycles as investors became greedy (because returns were great) and complacent (because downside risk appeared to be minimal or even nonexistent). Consequently, capacity and investments expanded exponentially. As a result too many canals and railroads were built. It is a relatively simple, though temporarily painful, process to liquidate excessive inventories. However, it is quite another task to liquidate a canal or railroad investment because it represents a basic piece of infrastructure. The capacity of such sizable capital investment projects can be worked off only over the course of many decades when demand eventually catches up with supply. More to the point, like all large infrastructure projects, they are impossible to construct without resorting to borrowed money. Consequently, part of the unwinding process involves paying down or writing off debt. Indeed, we can go so far as to say that pretty much all long-term downturns have their roots in careless bank lending practices, whether it is to industry, individuals, or real estate.

The canal and railroad booms started off with capital being allocated efficiently. As investors optimistically extrapolated continued boom conditions into the future, projects became more speculative and eventually a misallocation of capital occurred. In those three words—*misallocation of capital*—you have the crux of our modern-day secular financial excesses.

The Importance of the Misallocation of Capital in Economic Downturns

In any economy there is always a finite amount of capital available for productive projects, and the capitalistic market usually does a good, but certainly not perfect, job of allocating it. This is because capital, when adjusted for risk, is attracted to the places where it can obtain the best return. The problem is that when an investment theme initially does well, it encourages a wider universe of investors. As time moves on, the investment story becomes even more believable thus enticing others to join the fray, especially as the speculation becomes ever more compelling. Nothing attracts attention like success. Positive psychology becomes contagious, but unfortunately crowd behavior leads to careless decisions. Bankers fall all over themselves to lend money to investors who have not considered the consequences of a mania and the bubble bursting.

One of the key problems is that such booming industries attract a considerable amount of the capital, capital that could be used more productively elsewhere. If there was an infinite amount of capital, this would not be a problem because other industries also benefiting from new investment could carry the load when our boom industry collapses. However, the stark reality is the industry breeding the mania sucks in most of the available money, so other more deserving sectors are starved of investment. When the bubble pops, capital that would be available for other deserving projects evaporates, wealth is destroyed, and the entire economy is left poorer.

The Technology and Housing Booms as Root
Causes of the Current Secular Bear Market

After March 24, 2000, the U.S. equity market, which always looks ahead, began to focus on our current long-term structural problems. Initially the problem was the technology boom, which provided a classic example of misallocation of capital. You may recall how virtually any technology start-up could raise substantial amounts of money just based on an unproven concept or idea that had no record of revenue, cash flow, or profits. The fact that new speculative stock issues consistently became public and quickly went to huge premiums added further evidence that investors were losing common investment sense.

The subsequent bursting of the technology mania was just the opening salvo. A few years later more capital was misallocated, but this time in the home-building and construction industry. As the decade progressed, lending practices became more and more lax as it became possible for individuals to purchase houses in some cases with no money down. The justification for this was based on the idea that house prices never went down and would only continue to rise. Indeed, everyone assumed that the real estate price boom would continue forever. Bankers, not willing to be outdone by their rivals, loosened lending standards and joined the bandwagon and competition within the mortgage and financing industry thus further propelling the housing boom. Consequently, the pressure was on to grant loans. Traditionally lenders had qualified buyers fairly stringently as a protection against default. It was therefore in their self-interest to make sure that those buyers receiving loans were qualified. Just prior to the peak in the housing bubble, the practice of bundling mortgages and reselling them to institutional investors became very popular. This meant that there was less pressure to qualify buyers because once mortgages were sold, the loans would be someone else's responsibility. To make matters even worse, the loans were granted to people who lenders knew would have difficulty maintaining the repayment schedule. They were also made at higher interest rates and other less favorable terms to compensate for the additional risk. These were known as subprime loans because that is exactly what they were. Their proportion of total mortgages rose from a historical 8 percent to over 20 percent in 2004 through 2006.

Lax lending practices had two effects. First, they encouraged more building because there were more "qualified" and willing buyers—a classic example of misallocation of capital. Second, when the unthinkable did actually happen and house prices fell, many families were forced into foreclosure and bankruptcy. To others who were able to hang on it meant they were unable to move until prices recovered.

The Debt Time Bomb

Having already worked off a lot of the burden of the tech bubble, the adverse effect of lower real estate prices, and the foreclosure overhang, the U.S. economy faces a far bigger test, which is again emanating from the lending sector. This time our problem is the federal government, as more and more capital is being misallocated to this unproductive sector of the economy.

A little history is in order here. During World War II and in early postwar years the public was very cautious, expecting the Great Depression to return. As a result savings rates were high. By the same token public debt began to shrink as the World War II war machine was unwound and life got back to normal. In addition liquidity in the system built up to extremely high levels and the U.S. balance sheet was at one of its strongest levels ever. Unfortunately those good financial times did not last.

Government spending took off in the 1960s with the Vietnam War and the advent of the Great Society. Rather than deciding between the classic "guns or butter" spending alternatives, politicians appropriated funding for both guns *and* butter. Spending during that time was not identifiable with a single political party. Unfortunately, spending is a bipartisan disease since both Republican and Democratic administrations have been guilty of running ongoing federal deficits. A deficit per se is not necessarily a bad thing, just as it is appropriate for individuals to borrow if it is within their means to pay back the loan. The problem with the U.S. government and with many other countries is that borrowing has gotten out of control. It is not yet beyond the point of no return, but it is getting pretty close. Chart 1-1 for instance shows the percentage of U.S. debt relative to its GDP.

CHART 1-1 U.S. Government Debt as a Percentage of GDP, 1800–2011
The current U.S. government debt ratio is at an alarmingly high level and will stifle future economic growth.

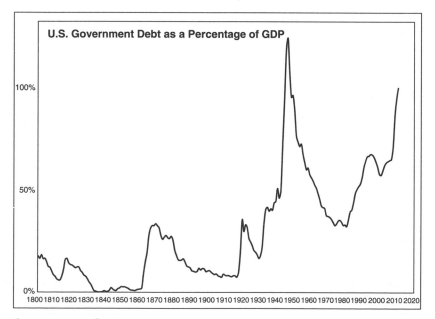

Source: treasurydirect.gov

Put another way, the government debt/GDP ratio is around 100 percent. Chart 1-2 shows that total debt, including the private sector, is much higher, but it may have peaked.

Remember, the accumulation of debt is the same thing as borrowing from the future for present consumption. Obligations incurred for investing in something productive, like plant or equipment, has the same future liability as borrowing for consumption. The big difference is that the investment is expected to produce something in the future. The vast majority of government borrowing is not for production but for current consumption, so when the consumption has taken place, the liability remains. At some point, when debt buildup becomes excessive, it is a drag on growth. In their book *This Time Is Different*, authors Carmen Reinhart and Kenneth Rogoff estimate

CHART 1-2 Total U.S. Debt (Public and Private) as a Percentage of GDP, 1900–2011

The total (public and private) debt deleveraging process is underway and will act to suppress economic growth for years to come.

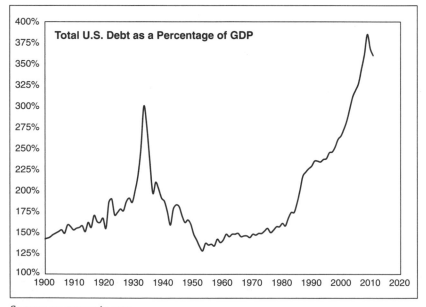

Source: economagic.com

that this moment arrives for any country when public debt reaches 90 percent of GDP. They demonstrate that when a country's gross government debt rises above this level, "The median growth rates fall by one percent and average growth falls considerably more." In this respect Table 1-1 presents the public, corporate, and household debt as a percentage of GDP for several leading countries. The picture is not a pretty one as the United States, Germany, Italy, and Japan are near or considerably above the 90 percent public debt threshold.

Furthermore, the U.S. debt clock (Figure 1-1) illustrates the extent of the government debt burden with more up-to-date figures than the 97 percent cited in Table 1-1. A January 2012 snapshot is shown in Figure 1-1 when the national debt stood at slightly over $15 trillion.

If we break the debt down into component pieces by showing debt per person, things become a little clearer. Bottom line: if you are a U.S. citizen, your share of debt is over *$48,400*. Not all citizens pay taxes, so the individual taxpayer is on the hook for *$134,500*! There is even more discouraging news from the debt clock when state and local governments, business, mortgage, credit card, and consumer debt are taken into consideration. This discouraging debt number is $56.4 trillion, or *$180,300* for every man, woman, and child in the United States.

TABLE 1-1 **Public, Corporate, and Household Debt as a Percentage of GDP for Selected Countries**
Many of the developed economies are suffering from the same excessive debt problem. This structural issue will take several business cycles to correct.

Debt Category	United States	Germany	Italy	Japan
Government	97%	77%	129%	213%
Nonfinancial				
Corporate	76%	100%	128%	161%
Household	75%	64%	53%	82%
Total % of GDP	248%	241%	310%	456%

Source: BIS Eurostat

FIGURE 1-1 U.S. Debt Clock, January 2012

The U.S. debt clock illustrates the unsustainable path the country is taking. Sooner or later a long-term solution must be found.

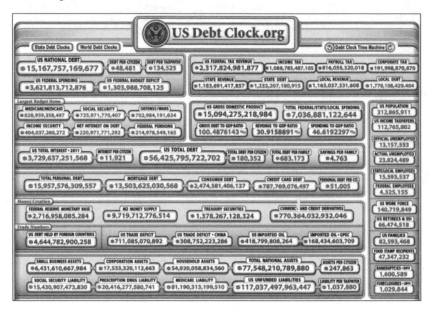

Source: usdebtclock.org

This is our problem today—simply too much debt. By the time you read this, these numbers will be out of date! To be fair, there are assets to be taken into consideration, and they amount to $247,000 per person. However, if you really want to play the numbers game, unfunded liabilities (promises with no money set aside to keep them), we are looking at *$1,037,882* per person!

The Keynesian model economic advisors and government officials have used since the 1940s calls for the government to run deficits during recessions and surpluses in good times. The intention of those surpluses is to restore fiscal sanity by paying down obligations incurred during the recession. Politicians took to heart only the first half of Keynesian theory that justified deficits and skipped the second more important half.

Debt can be likened to drug addiction. The longer you take drugs, the more you need in order to get to that same high and the worse the withdrawal symptoms are when you want or are forced to kick the habit. Drug addiction is subject to the law of diminishing returns; so is borrowing. For example, you could say that you want to purchase a 1 percent increase in GDP by borrowing a dollar to do it. There's not a lot wrong with that. However, as the borrowing load has increased, it has taken an increasing number of dollars to buy one unit of GDP. The most recent number we have is that it takes $6 of debt to generate $1 worth of growth. The marginal returns for increasing debt to generate growth have reached a terminal level.

To help put these extraordinarily large sums into perspective, we offer a simple analogy. Let us assume that the members of our Smith family ran their household finances the same way the federal government runs its finances. In order to make the numbers more believable, we knock off a few zeros so we can relate and can get a better understanding of government's financial mismanagement. Imagine that this past year the Smiths earned (tax revenue) $23,178 and spent $36,218. The $13,040 of overspending (deficit) was charged to their credit card that already had a balance of $151, 678 (total debt) or nearly seven times the Smiths' annual income. Would you say that the Smiths have a big debt problem? Of course you would. Today, interest rates are low, but what happens to the Smiths' budget if interest rates were to climb even just a few percentage points? A two or three percentage increase from today's record low interest rates would easily add $3,000 to $4,000 to the Smiths' deficit each year and compound their debt even faster. Now add eight zeros to these numbers, and instead of thousands we are talking *trillions of dollars*, and you have a better perspective on how irresponsible the U.S. federal government runs its household budget! This budget does not work for the Smiths, and it does not work for the U.S. government. This is clearly an unsustainable direction which

TABLE 1-2 U.S. Federal Debt Outstanding
The trend in U.S. federal debt is accelerating higher, which is
a dilemma that will have to be addressed in the next decade.

Year	Debt (Trillions)	Annual Growth Rate
2000	5.8	N/A
2004	7.0	4.8%
2008	9.3	7.4%
2012	15.2	13.1%
2015*	23.9*	16.3%

*Estimated based on current debt trends.
Source: usdebtclock.org

sooner rather than later has to be addressed, and remedies have to be
found.

If you want to peek into the future, the debt clock lets you do so,
and some of the data are featured in Table 1-2.

There are two things to note. First, the debt is increasing; second, it
is growing at a faster and faster rate. U.S. federal debt started off with
a 4.8 percent annual growth rate between 2000 and 2004, rising to a
13.1 percent annual growth rate between 2005 and 2012. The annual
growth rate is projected to reach 16.3 percent between 2012 and 2015.
We are on a collision course. At some point this debt expansion will
become unsustainable. A car constantly increasing its rate of acceleration is certain to crash unless the brakes are applied or a foot is taken
off the gas pedal. So too is an economy based on accelerating debt
accumulation.

What, If Any, Are the Solutions? What Are the
Implications for the Secular Bear Market?

There are really only three solutions to the debt problem, all of which
imply a significant extension to the secular bear market that started
on March 24, 2000. The first would be a dramatic reduction in the

deficit. This reduction could be achieved by raising taxes or cutting spending or a combination of both. Given the scale of the deficit—approximately $1.5 trillion at the start of 2012—even a 30 to 50 percent cut would involve huge pain and certainly act as a substantial negative drag on the economy. In the long run this would be a positive step as it would reallocate assets from the (unproductive) public to the (productive) private sector. A second solution would be for the government to write down, or default on, some of its debt. Taking this course, though, would result in the loss of the country's already recently lowered AA credit rating. A write down of any kind would immediately push U.S. bonds toward junk bond status with junk-sized interest rates to go with it. The implications of a severe downgrade along with the financial pain inflicted on creditors would most certainly hamstring the economy. The third possibility, and the one most used by governments so cornered, is to start up the printing presses and inflate out of the debt mess by creating more money. As you will see in later chapters, one of the characteristics of secular bear markets is unstable rates of commodity price inflation. If the government succeeds in inflating its way out of the problem, you can be sure there would be instability and therefore destruction in the purchasing value of the U.S. dollar and most equities.

The final possibility is to grow the economy out of the debt quagmire. Growth is another way of raising taxes, but it is a much more beneficial one, since people pay more to the government, not because of a tax-rate increase but because they get to earn, keep, and pay more taxes, but at the same rate. Thus both government and taxpayer win. So how does an economy grow its way out of a problem?

First, government would need to take immediate steps to improve confidence, because when people are confident, they are much more willing to spend and invest. Confidence would be boosted by a serious plan involving spending restraints. In Washington a cut refers to only a slowdown in spending, whereas in the real world a cut actually means less spending. Washington needs to get real. Other obvious steps would involve a serious plan attacking unnecessary and costly regulations. For instance, relaxing oil and gas drilling regulations, freeing up bandwidth for easier telecommunications, reducing or even eliminating quotas on qualified foreigners, yes the kind of entrepreneurial ones that started up Intel, and yes those companies employing tens of thousands of employees. New York is rapidly losing its predominance as a financial center, and it is true that this is partially the result of the natural global transition to Asia. But why help this process along with well-meaning but job killing, stifling regulatory bills like Sarbanes-Oxley and Dodd-Frank? Keep the good parts and repeal the bad ones. Capital always migrates to where it is treated best.

Most important of all we come back to the subject of misallocation of capital. Arguably the most significant cause of inefficient capital allocation lies in the tax code. Lobbyists pay elected government officials through campaign donations for special favors in the form of tax incentives or exceptions for their industry. As a result we are left with unnecessary tax complications and misallocation of resources. It is like putting a dam at the edge of a fertile field and allowing a trickle of water to fertilize the crops while the owner of the dam swims, fishes, and boats in a nice deep lake. Eliminating the dam and letting the water flow freely through the irrigation channels might cause some problems for the dam owner but it would certainly increase the agricultural productivity for everyone else.

Constant changes in the tax code also result in uncertainty and the inability of businesses to make solid plans. The future is always uncertain, but why not help reduce some of this uncertainty by putting in place a reform of the tax code that phases out all loopholes, tax expenditures, or whatever you want to call them, and simultaneously lowers tax rates. Both corporate and individual tax codes would be included, and the bill would include a clause requiring a two-thirds majority of both houses to permit an amendment. Another idea would reduce corporate tax rates if a corporation adopted a government-approved profit plan. One of the principles of these plans would limit the amount of the salary multiple of top executives relative to lowly paid workers. Another would offer shareholders some protection against unscrupulous management. Everyone would gain from such an arrangement—shareholders, workers, and management. The icing on the cake would be a reduction in the degree of inequality and sense of injustice. Unfortunately, most of these possibilities involve the application of common sense, a virtue lacking in most politicians.

However, we can leave you with some positive trends that are taking place under the radar and will come into fruition in the next decade or so. We talked earlier about the tech boom and bust and the exponential rise in the debt, but there is exponential growth going on elsewhere and that is in the technology sector. For instance, Moore's law states the long-term trend in the history of computing hardware is that the number of transistors that can be placed inexpensively on an integrated circuit doubles approximately every 18 months. In his book *The Singularity Is Near* (Viking, 2005), futurist Ray Kurzweil calls this the law of accelerating returns because, as he points out, this principle applies to many different sectors of technology. He argues that the ever-accelerating rate of technological change will soon mean that computers will rival the full range of human intelligence at its best. In *Singularity* he poses an era in which our intelligence will become increasingly nonbiological and trillions of times more powerful. There is that "trillion" word again, but this time in a much more favorable light. As an example, nanotechnology will make it possible to create virtually any physical product using inexpensive information processes. The productivity gains will be limitless. To the doubters among you, it took about 50 years for the late-nineteenth-century innovation called the telephone to reach a significant usage level. Compare this to the late twentieth century, which took less than a decade for the cell phone to achieve the same goal. There are many other examples of this exponential technological takeoff.

Imagine the effect on healthcare as the latest technology is used to further map out the human genome leading to medications and cures to our most dreaded diseases.

Perhaps the area with the most exciting potential is in the energy arena where technological improvements like horizontal drilling and "hydrofracking," a process to optimize the extraction of oil and natural gas from oil fields. These new techniques are definitely shaping up to be big-time game changers. This new technology is allowing for the continued explosive development of U.S. oil production taking place in North Dakota's expansive Bakken oil shale formation. Continental Resources, the largest leaseholder and most active driller, declared in January 2011 that the formation could become the world's largest onshore discovery of the last 30 to 40 years with the ultimate recovery potential of 24 billion barrels. This rich resource has already powered North Dakota ahead of OPEC member Ecuador in total oil production. Further, Goldman Sachs has estimated that by 2017 the United States will move from being the world's number three oil producer behind Russia and Saudi Arabia to the number one spot!

The point here is not that we should totally ignore our financial problems but that there is substantial evidence in favor of a very positive outlook down the road. Many branches of technology, for instance, are reaching their "knee of the curve" jump-off positions or the exponential takeoff point of no return. It is Kurzweil's expectation that these developments are not far away in terms of time. Perhaps they're not close enough to avoid the second lost decade, but they will probably arrive in time to fuel the next secular bull market.

Our investment view is determined by *historical* financial observations, *current* equity and fixed income overvaluations, and *future* solutions to the spiraling debt problem. The solutions will not be painless. The combination of past, present, and future economic and financial observations are different from humanity's march of progress. Progress will not be stopped by a temporary retreat in financial markets— even a 10- or 20-year retreat. When equity markets have recognized and adjusted for debt resolutions and valuations are low enough, we will be in position to begin the next secular bull market. It will arrive just in time to usher in the future financial golden age wherein investors will catch up with all of the standard-of-living advances made during the stock market's lost decades. This book teaches you how to survive; keep your financial health intact; and enjoy the higher wealth, health, and happiness certain to happen. Good investing!

KEY POINTS

1. Typical cyclical economic downturns correct the excesses of the prior expansion. Secular bear periods correct the deeper, *structural* excesses.
2. The misallocation of resources (for instance, housing overinvestment) is a root cause of secular bear periods.
3. The debt deleveraging process ultimately means we face years of slower economic growth and the potential for more and deeper recessions.
4. There are solutions to budget and debt issues, but we need the political will to tackle them before they tackle us.
5. The United States has a splendid history of innovation, technological breakthrough, and perseverance that always lead to ever-increasing standards of living. This period is no different.

IMPORTANT QUESTIONS FROM THE SMITHS

How are we going to invest profitably in the meantime, before all these exciting things take effect?

One way is to follow the principles we outline later. The first step is to recognize that there actually is a structural problem and not be lulled into a false sense of security by those around you or in the media. Expectations are an important factor in investing, so if you assume returns on stocks and bonds over a 5- to 10-year period are likely to be subpar, you can change tactics to handle the environment. As always in secular bear markets there will be 1- to 3-year rallies, or cyclical bull markets, that provide great investment opportunities. But do not forget that the secular bear will eventually resume its destructive path, so having a serious game plan to play defense during the cyclical bad periods is critical to preserving your nest egg. No one can predict when the current secular bear will end, but in Chapter 3 and Appendix A we provide some guidelines as to what the end of previous downtrends have looked like. We would strongly recommend that you assume that the secular bear is still in force until some of these benchmarks come into view.

CHAPTER 2

WHAT ARE SECULAR TRENDS IN STOCKS AND WHY DO THEY MATTER TO YOU?

The time horizon for most investors has shrunk a great deal in the last 40 years or so. The reasons lie in the widespread use of computers and the easy availability of instant news analysis and data via the Internet. The technology may make us feel informed and in control of the situation, but it's less empowering when it comes to performance. Performance suffers because the emotions of people who are constantly watching the news and the latest quotes are being continuously stimulated. As a result, the tendency is to make subjective assessments based on knee-jerk reactions. Decisions made by successful investors, on the other hand, tend to be far more objective.

The other handicap experienced by the screen-watching generation is loss of perspective. Experienced mountain climbers would never think of attempting an assault on Mount Everest at the start of winter because they would realize that bad weather would doom their chances. In this instance their decision-making process would rely on the perspective of the seasons. You would be amazed, though, at how many investors expose themselves to equities just as a big bad bear market is about to begin. They do this simply because they have chosen to ignore the perspective of long-term trends. Buying stocks in a bear market is like paddling a canoe up the rapids. It can be done theoretically but you would use so much energy that the whole process would be counterproductive. The 24/7 business news media have almost completely ignored long-term trends in favor of trading strategies. In a similar manner investors today have, to a large extent, lost their sense of perspective. We try to break that mold in this chapter by studying some extremely long-term charts in order to get a better understanding of the perspective they provide.

What Are Secular and Business Cycle Trends?

Throughout the book we promise not to be overly technical and boring, but we do need to put a couple of definitions on the table so you can see where we are coming from. First, a *trend* is a period in which a price moves in an irregular but persistent direction. Trends that revolve around the four- to five-year business cycle are known as *cyclical trends*. When people refer to "bull" and "bear" markets or the *primary trend* they are usually talking about these cyclical swings. *Secular trends* are very long term in nature and embrace several business cycles. These trends develop both positively and negatively, and they average around 20 years in duration. However, some secular trends can be as short as a decade, and others have been known to extend for 40 years or more. Secular trends develop in stock, bond, and commodity markets. We will look at the secular price movements for bonds and commodities in later chapters, but for now our focus is on equities.

In the very long run, stock prices go up. We are not going to argue this truism. However, since recorded financial history began, and for the U.S. stock market that means around 1800, stock prices have alternated between secular bull (good) and bear (bad) markets. "Secular" in this sense refers to a *very long-term trend* in prices extending over several business cycles.

Before we go any further, let us expand on what we mean by the term *business cycle* since we use this phrase a lot. It refers to the normal four- to five-year ebb and flow of the economy reflecting the constant fluctuations in the level of economic activity between growth and contraction. Essentially the business cycle is a reflection of market psychology—the alternation between caution, optimism, greed, and fear. Figure 2-1 shows that a typical business cycle starts with economic recovery, leading to growth acceleration, and then a peak in economic activity. This is followed by a growth slowdown, leading to a contraction, and if severe, back into a recession. History shows that the cycle repeats on average every four to five years—the average for all cycles since 1854 is roughly 55 months.

If you have had a job in a cyclical industry like home building, the auto industry, or any other heavy manufacturing industry, you

FIGURE 2-1 **The Sequential Nature of the Business Cycle**
The repetitive ebb and flow of the business cycle reflects the constant fluctuation in the economy.

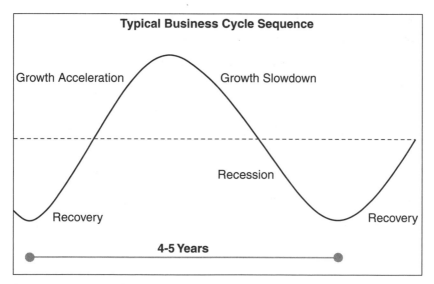

Source: Pring Turner Capital Group

probably remember the effects of these typical boom and bust periods. You are probably well aware of the business cycle on a very personal level. However, those employed in the healthcare, utility, or government sectors have little firsthand experience with the normal four- to five-year swings in the economy. They may have to take a little extra time to fully understand the effects of the business cycle on their everyday life and investment portfolio. In later chapters, we will elaborate on business cycles and their usefulness not only in the investment world but in many other aspects of your everyday life. This includes helping with decisions such as when to buy a car or refinance a mortgage or whether to expand a business or not. For now, it is important to understand that secular good and bad periods for stocks are made up of a string of four- to five-year business cycles. In this respect Figure 2-2 shows how trends in equity prices influenced by the business cycle revolve around these very long-term or secular ones.

To understand the differences between secular bull and bear markets, let's return to our retirement couple, the Smiths. As we mentioned, secular trends often last 20 years or more. Since they alternate between secular bull and secular bear, most investors will experience both in their 40 to 50 year investment horizon. A typical investment lifetime would include two phases. First, an *accumulation* period between, say, ages 40 and 65, where assets are being built up through savings. The other is a *distribution* stage during retirement between ages 65 and 90, where the accumulated assets are consumed. Like many other couples, the Smiths accumulated their sizable retirement nest egg during the fabulous secular bull market of the 1980s and 1990s. Steady contributions into 401(k) and other employer retirement programs along with two decades of above-average, double-digit returns built their retirement balances progressively and relatively effortlessly. Payroll deductions into mutual funds allowed for the sensible

FIGURE 2-2 How Business Cycle Trends Fit into Secular Trends
A secular trend is formed when a series of business cycles are linked together establishing long periods of stock market outperformance and underperformance.

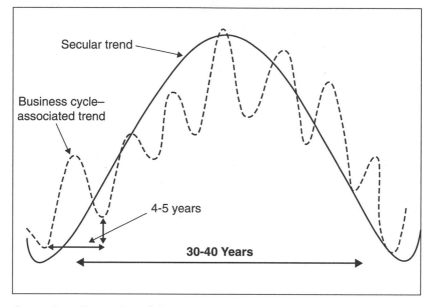

Source: Pring Turner Capital Group

dollar cost averaging strategy to work its magic and compound steadily. Any market setbacks were relatively mild and were followed by quick recoveries to new highs. Looking back, it is easy to say in large part that much of the thanks for their success in building a sizable nest egg can be given to the secular bull market environment they were fortunate enough to fully participate in. If only the positive environment could stay the same forever, but history tells us that investors cannot extrapolate this positive trend forever into the future.

Instead, stocks alternate between good and bad secular periods about every 20 years or so. And each period requires a completely different mindset and game plan for success. As a result, many investors are woefully ill-prepared for the new environment at these major secular turning points, and they suffer consequences. One goal in this book is to provide you with the investment tools useful for the purpose of identifying the direction of the secular trend and to enable you to position yourself with the appropriate investment strategy to survive and prosper, no matter what the background environment. Understanding the current secular environment is critical to your ultimate success or failure as an investor, and our belief is that many have not even taken long-term trends into consideration.

Having some understanding of the direction of the prevailing secular trend is important because *secular trends dominate the characteristics of cyclical trends,* just as climate dominates the seasons. Both Montreal and Miami experience seasons, but their differing climates dominate how severe their winters will be. It is the same in the financial markets. Remember, the tide of a secular bull market lifts all boats as investors are quickly bailed out of their mistakes. On the other hand, anyone who adopts the buy-hold approach might be a temporary hero, but the secular bear ultimately proves that the emperor has no clothes.

Risky strategies may work in a secular bull market, but the timely use of defensive cautious strategies will enable you to preserve real purchasing power during a secular bear. This is because bullish cyclical trends in a rising secular trend are persistent and have substantial magnitude, while cyclical bear trends are typically short and shallow. The opposite is true during a secular bear market, where cyclical bull markets *tend* to be shorter and limited in scope, and the business cycle associated with bear markets tends to be far more severe.

You will notice that we emphasize the word tend because that is what happens the majority of the time. However, markets are driven more by psychology than fundamentals, so the unpredictability of the human psyche comes into play a lot more than most would suspect.

Investing in a secular trend is just like sailing. In a secular bull market the investment wind is behind you. It is virtually impossible not to make progress. On the other hand, in a secular bear market the wind is coming at you full force, which means that the going will be much more difficult. In sailing it is still possible to get to your destination by tacking, but it is a much more onerous task and requires some degree of skill. In the case of a secular bear market in equities, the money management skill required is the tactical rotation and allocation of assets as the cycle progresses. This may sound like a bit of a mouthful, but we will break that one down in later chapters in the sections devoted to money management techniques utilizing business cycle analysis.

Secular Trends in U.S. Equities Since 1800

They say that a picture is worth a thousand words, and we believe that a carefully selected chart is worth a thousand pictures. Chart 2-1 shows the course of the U.S. stock market since 1800. The solid and

CHART 2-1 U.S. Stock Prices (S&P Composite Since 1926), 1800–2011
In the long run stock prices go up, but there are alternating secular good and bad periods that can last two decades or more.

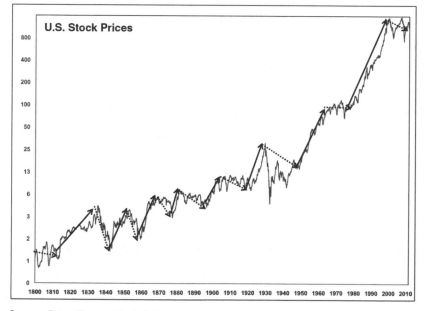

Source: Pring Turner Capital Group

dashed arrows approximate the secular trends in this nominal price series—that is prices that are *not* adjusted for inflation.

For sure, in the very long run it is readily evident that stock prices go up. The chart is evidence for buy-and-hold believers that all an investor needs to do is let the long-term uptrend in stock prices take its course. This is true if you live long enough and if you have time to make it to the next secular *bull* period.

Upon more careful observation, a couple of turning points may look inconsistent, such as the 1949 low being used instead of the actual low in 1932. Please bear with us as an explanation will follow later. Some of you may also be questioning the 1900–1921 and 1966–1982 periods as "bear" markets when prices looked to be in a relatively nonthreatening trading range. The answer will become clear to you later when we look at these time periods on an *inflation-adjusted* basis.

Why is inflation important? It is because inflation is the stealth tax on wealth. From an investor's long-term perspective real purchasing power is more important than absolute prices. You may see the value of your portfolio jump by 15 percent but if inflation takes away 20 percent, you are actually 5 percent worse off in the amount of goods your portfolio can purchase, and that does not even take into account the taxes you owe on your "gain." Inflation erodes returns. It is because the damage in real purchasing power is a serious issue that we prefer to express stock prices in inflation-adjusted terms when considering secular trends. Another reason is that inflation-adjusted prices make these long-term pendulum swings easier to spot. After taking a look at Chart 2-2, which shows the stock market since 1870 adjusted for inflation, you can quickly appreciate the *damage inflation and secular bear markets wreak on a portfolio's purchasing power.*

CHART 2-2 U.S. Stock Prices (S&P Composite Spliced) Adjusted for Inflation, 1870–2011

Inflation-adjusted prices make the secular good and bad periods easier to identify. Currently we are in the middle of the fourth secular bear market since 1870.

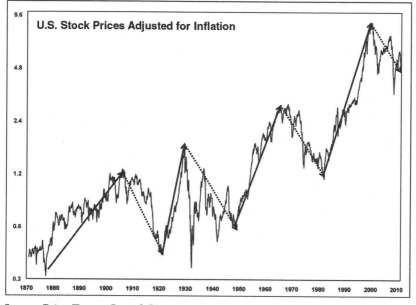

Source: Pring Turner Capital Group

Now the secular bull and bear trends are much more apparent as the chart makes clear that the 1900–1921 and 1966–1982 "trading ranges" were really a disaster for stock investors as returns after inflation were sharply negative. Note that the year 2000 saw the onset of the fourth secular bear market since 1900. By early 2012, it was over 12 years old. Based on the historical duration of previous U.S. secular bears of around 19 years, there will be much more downside action to experience in the second decade of the century.

The Characteristics of Secular Bulls Versus Secular Bear Markets

In the next chapter we will take a look at the kinds of things to be on the lookout for at secular turning points for equities. Prior to that though, it makes sense to more closely examine the characteristics of both up- and downtrends. Secular bull markets are enjoyable for everyone because corrections are short and shallow, and each successive peak is higher than its predecessor. They definitely reinforce the belief that a rising tide lifts all boats, which in a practical sense means that investors are repeatedly bailed out from their mistakes. As a result, confidence builds over an extended period and grows to excessive levels at the peak. At that point investors think themselves to be investment geniuses. Remember when you were in a similar state of mind where everything moved in your favor? You can see why decisions, considered to be irresponsible and careless at the start of the trend, are hailed as perfectly acceptable as the secular bull market matures. The old conservative rule book, learned at great expense during the previous secular bear market, is thrown out as investors embrace the new era thinking that "this time is different."

Secular bears are characterized by lower equity peaks and troughs in successive business cycles as real purchasing value is slowly and painfully eaten away. Secular bulls lend themselves admirably to the buy-hold approach, but an entirely different strategy is appropriate as the secular bear unfolds. Under this abusive environment, offensive tactics during the relatively brief cyclical bull markets that run counter to the secular downdraft help to slowly build wealth. These kinds of conditions necessitate portfolios being protected by defensive tactics because of the devastating declines that take place when the secular bear resumes.

One of the early results of a secular bear is to expose careless mistakes, financial excesses, and the inevitable fraud that accompanies the aftermath of a long-term boom period. Witness the examples of corporate fraud in Enron, WorldCom, and the enormous Ponzi scheme contrived by the infamous Bernie Madoff. In April 2003 we originally published an article on www.pring.com (which you can read at www.pringturner.com) that posed the question, "Whither the Secular Trend of Equities?" This piece laid out the case for the year 2000 being a secular or very long-term peak for the U.S. stock market. The article forecast that equity prices would experience a wide multiyear trading range as sentiment unwound from the unrealistic assumptions that pushed price/earnings ratios and dividend yields to record extremes. Since that peak, equities have been unable to make any net progress and have lost considerable value in purchasing power terms. You may be wondering if enough time has elapsed to justify a reversion back to a buy-hold approach or whether the tactical asset allocation strategy that served our clients so well in the opening year of the century is no longer appropriate. Unfortunately, the evidence indicates that the current secular bear is likely to ravage investors' portfolios well into the mid-decade and probably to 2020 and beyond. We can't tell you exactly when the next secular bull market will begin because there are no known techniques suitable for consistently forecasting the duration of price moves in financial markets. However, we can tell you what sort of things to look out for based on what transpired at previous secular lows. By the time you have finished reading Chapter 3, you should have a pretty good idea of what the end of a secular bear looks like. To help you on your way, we will give you a simple checklist of what to monitor.

We hope that you are now in a better position to appreciate the mindless focus on intraday trading and instant news, and the importance of understanding the larger more powerful forces that dominate the bigger trends. The crucial question is, what causes stock prices to undergo these long-term phases of good and bad fortune? *We think there are two primary forces driving secular trends: investor psychology and excessive movements (in either direction) of commodity prices caused by long-term structural imbalances of the type outlined in the previous chapter.* This is the topic for Chapter 3.

KEY POINTS

1. Secular trends entail long periods of alternating good and bad market performance.
2. Secular trends (20+ years) are the result of several business cycle swings (4 to 5 years) strung together.
3. Long-term trend changes since 1800 can be identified viewing history in both absolute and inflation-adjusted terms.
4. The current secular bear market for stocks is likely to last about another decade.

IMPORTANT QUESTIONS FROM THE SMITHS

If there is another lost decade for equities, should we avoid equities altogether?

No, there will still be cyclical stock market opportunities, such as those between 2003 and 2007 and 2009 and 2012, where investors can build wealth safely. But, just as important, investors need a defensive game plan to protect wealth during the cyclical declines. Subsequent chapters provide the building blocks for navigating through the second lost decade for stocks.

CHAPTER 3

WHAT FORCES CAUSE SECULAR TRENDS IN EQUITY PRICES? WHAT DO THE TURNING POINTS LOOK LIKE?

Stock prices are determined by people's attitudes to the emerging fundamentals rather than the fundamentals themselves. That's because investors anticipate future developments and factor them into prices several months ahead of time. This involves a certain amount of guessing and comparison of potential equity returns to competing assets such as bonds, commodities, or even real estate. Stocks "do not sell for what they are worth but for what people think they are worth," as the legendary Wall Street analyst Garfield Drew once observed. If you have ever studied political polls, you will notice that they move in trends as whatever is being polled, be it issues or individuals, is continually shifting from a low level of acceptance to a high one and vice versa. Markets are the same in that they are continually moving in and out of fashion as investors alternate between excessive optimism and greed at tops and fear and panic at bottoms. Secular trends are no different except to say the forces are much stronger and reflect far greater magnitude and duration in their mood swings than trends, say, associated with the business cycle.

Psychological and Structural Aspects of Secular Bear Markets

If long-term swings in equity prices were driven by the fundamentals then you would expect to see fluctuations in stock prices associated with changes in corporate profitability. Long-term swings in inflation-adjusted profits and equity prices would then be expected to move pretty well in tandem. That sounds logical doesn't it? Chart 3-1 clearly shows this relationship to be a myth, as profits have actually increased during the three secular bear markets that occurred since 1900. This is also true in the twenty-first century, where stocks in early 2012 were down from their 2000 peak despite profits (at the latest reporting period at year end 2011) reaching new all-time highs.

We are not saying that profitability and prices are totally disconnected because there is usually a far closer relationship so far as

CHART 3-1 Inflation-Adjusted U.S. Stock Prices Versus Shiller Real Earnings, 1870–2011
Stock prices can continue to face secular headwinds despite rising corporate earnings.

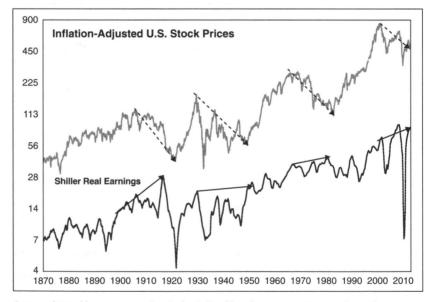

Source: http://www.econ.yale.edu/~shiller/data.htm; Pring Turner Capital Group

swings associated within the business cycle are concerned. However, this is clearly not so for very long-term time trends, which, as we have stated, are more a function of psychology than economics. An understanding of the secular trend therefore is an appreciation of the fact that investors are continually undergoing long-term psychological mood swings, similar to the swing of a pendulum in a grandfather clock. Stocks, like a lot of things, move in and out of fashion. For example, short hair for men was popular in the 1950s; long hair was popular in the later 1960s and 1970s. At the start of the twenty-first century fully shaven heads grew in popularity. The alternation between high and low hemlines for women's fashion is legendary. Stocks are no different.

To understand the nature of secular price movements in equities, we need to take into consideration the fact that the longer a specific trend or condition exists, the more mentally ingrained it becomes in us. Investors are cautious at the start of a secular bull market because they are mindful of the previous bear market disaster. Eventually they gain confidence, as each successive business cycle–associated bull market rewards them. This process extends as investors gradually lower their guard, sooner or later falling victim to careless decisions as they are sucked in by their own success and egged on by an ever more optimistic crowd around them. When the trend actually does reverse, a dramatic correction follows. The secular bear market is not caused by these careless investment decisions because such decisions can be quickly and painfully corrected by the cleansing process of a cyclical bear market and deep recession.

The *secular bear* is more structural in nature. Typically a specific industry or economic sector will gain in popularity during the previous secular bull, often as a result of technological innovation. This results in a misallocation of capital culminating in the formation of substantial excess capacity, way more than that seen at a normal cyclical peak. For example, let us say that the housing industry has the capacity to produce 1.5 million homes a year and normally sells about 1.2 million. Let us also say that a recession causes sales to fall to 1 million homes, while inventories of unsold homes climb. Naturally, home builders slow down the building pipeline to absorb excess inventory. In the subsequent economic recovery, sales rebound back to 1.2 million, inventories are absorbed, and a new growth cycle can take place. It means that the industry has taken a temporary hit and has rebounded. This represents a great example of a cyclical problem that proves to be temporary. On the other hand, if during the latest recovery (as occurred in the lead up to the 2007 housing bubble) capacity grows to over 2.2 million new homes built each year based on unrealized expectations of future growth, that is a *structural* problem. It is structural because this huge surplus of capacity (and large inventory of unsold new homes) will remain during the course of the next recovery because sales could not possibly rise sufficiently to clear out the excess inventory. It will obviously require several such cycles to work off the excess.

Secular bear markets are characterized by these structural or long-term distortions that have their roots in the prosperous times of the previous secular bull. Indeed, we can go further by stating that each secular bull is characterized by its own excesses. For example, it was canals in the early part of the nineteenth century, railroads in the 1870s, manufacturing in 1929, electronics in the 1960s, dot-com in 1999, housing in 2007, and so forth. One of the by-products of a skyrocketing stock market is the ability of firms to raise cheap capital. This not only results in risky mergers and acquisitions but also results in excess capacity. Companies are therefore precluded from fully recovering until this surplus has been worked off or written down. This cheap capital causes two problems. First, because specific industries are in fashion, they can attract huge amounts of capital regardless of the companies' merits. Remember all those dot-com companies that came public in the very late 1990s and easily raised new money from willing investors? Some of those companies are still with us, but most have gone bust. Second, there is a limited amount of capital available at any one time. This means that if undeserving enterprises are receiving capital, other more worthwhile projects are not.

A key characteristic of a secular bull, with its backdrop of growing confidence, is the slow but deliberate nurturing of fraudulent behavior. This is masked during the great investment boom, just like the fact that termites are not visibly apparent until substantial rot has set in. Fraud in markets becomes apparent only later on, when prices "unexpectedly" start to slip and credit is no longer available. At that time such schemes and scams are quickly exposed.

Governments and financial institutions play their part, of course, as the stringent rules developed as a legacy of the previous bear are gradually relaxed during the uptrend and then rigorously reapplied during the subsequent downtrend, when it is too late. A key recent example might be the gradual easing of rules for mortgage approvals that helped fuel the speculative real estate boom and subsequent crash. One of the structural problems associated with the second phase of the 2000–20?? secular bear is the need to work or write off much of that debt.

Once the cycle turns over, the rush to find scapegoats supersedes common sense and prudence. Politicians are a lagging indicator, so it is natural for them to respond to the unrest fomented by the downtrend. The problem is that these knee-jerk reactions lead to policy mistakes, which though intended to help, usually make the situation worse. Higher taxes, the Smoot-Hawley tariff, and competitive devaluations were all characteristics of 1930s style of policy errors. Others would argue that in more recent times the Sarbanes-Oxley and Dodd-Frank acts did far more harm than good in their problem-solving abilities, but at least government could be seen to be doing *something*.

In addition, since the 2008 banking crisis reared its ugly head, part of the current secular bear will be plagued with the problem of a historic debt overhang, which is when the level of existing debt is so great that it is not easy, or is even impossible, to borrow or service additional debt. Such a condition will substantially inhibit the normal cyclical growth that typically follows recession. The prospect of massive tax increases looms as an additional potential policy mistake. As for distortions, government policy during the immediate post–2008 crisis period moved to prop up the housing market with special credits and more difficult foreclosure regulations. The correct thing to do would be to let prices drop and clear the excess supply. Obviously that would have been more painful at the time but would have quickly solved the root problem—oversupply. Instead, the process dragged on, arguably causing more pain in the long run. Just consider the situation of a patient taking pills to stop the *symptoms* of her illness rather than undergoing the immediate and greater pain of a surgery that would actually *cure* her medical problem. Absent a course correction, bankrupt Medicare and Social Security entitlements represent icing on the secular bearish cake. Individuals are already working to solve these kinds of problems by restructuring their balance sheets, paying off debt, and getting on with life on a more sensible footing. Unfortunately, until political solutions begin to move in that direction, government policies will likely be providing additional fuel to the secular bear trend.

Valuation and Investor Sentiment

The price-to-earnings or P/E ratio is calculated by simply dividing the price (P) of a company by the earnings per share (E). The P/E ratio represents how much an investor is willing to pay for one dollar's worth of earnings. The P/E ratio measures investor confidence. It is one of the most popular valuation yardsticks used for stocks. As prices decline, P/E ratios fall and indicate better value as investor concerns intensify. Secular bull markets begin with investor attitudes reflecting low confidence, fear, disgust, and exceptionally subdued expectations as reflected in very low P/E ratios. This attitude is widespread after investors experience the prior 20-year secular bear market that slowly grinds away their confidence. On the other hand, secular bear markets begin after a 20-year runaway bull period that takes investor confidence to extremely high levels. P/E ratios follow by ratcheting higher and higher with confidence levels increasing, and reflect the overvalued, overowned, and overexuberant atmosphere. Relating this to our most recent history, the 18-year period from 1982 to 2000 embraced the last secular bull market. Stocks were grossly overvalued, and investors were wildly optimistic with unrealistic expectations at the conclusion of this secular bull. Since 2000, we have embarked on a much different and far less investor-friendly journey, which probably represents only the first half of the secular bear market.

Let us take a look at investor sentiment around these secular turning points more closely. With the benefit of over 150 years of financial history, it is possible to establish benchmarks that tell us when valuations have reached excessive levels that are consistent with the optimistic extremes reached at secular turning points.

We have established that a secular peak is one that culminates in a very long-term advance encompassing several (business cycle–associated) bull markets. By their very nature such market turning points involve the kind of overconfidence among investors that is rarely seen and not repeated for a generation at least. In effect, it is necessary for secular peaks and troughs to be separated by sufficient time so that investors forget the mistakes of the past and are therefore in an ideal position to repeat them. These secular-trend turning points in the stock market can most easily be recognized by extremes in valuation measures. Indeed, secular trends in equity prices could well be described as very long-term swings in over- and undervaluation. During this process investors' attitudes move from excessive and irrational optimism to unjustified pessimism, where disgust with equities becomes so widespread that at the end of the trend few are willing to own them.

Secular bear markets are characterized by several factors. The most important is the complete reversal in psychology from the euphoria and overconfidence of the previous secular bull to one of total disgust with equities by the time the bear has run its course. Unfortunately this is not an overnight process but requires prices to experience a huge drop over an extended time period. The magnitude aspect is especially apparent after consideration is given to the real purchasing value of equities. The lengthy and substantial decline is extremely discouraging to investors as they see their wealth slowly erode. It is the extended duration of the drop in real purchasing power that eats away the confidence of even the most optimistic investors. Experience has shown that in order to correct the structural distortions built up in the previous secular bull, it has been typical for the economy to undergo between four and six deeper and longer-than-normal recessions before the secular bear is finally laid to rest.

We will examine the psychological aspects first by considering valuation, not as a fundamental measure but as one of sentiment. Arguably the most popular long-term measure of stock market valuation is the price investors are willing to pay for corporate earnings. In this respect please take a moment to look at the Shiller P/E series at the bottom of Chart 3-2.

Noted economist and professor Robert Shiller uses a proprietary 10-year average P/E ratio to smooth out the volatile business cycle

CHART 3-2 Inflation-Adjusted U.S. Stock Prices Versus the Shiller Price/
Earnings Ratio,* 1900–2011

The current secular bear market is only half over. Secular bear markets end at very
low valuation levels.

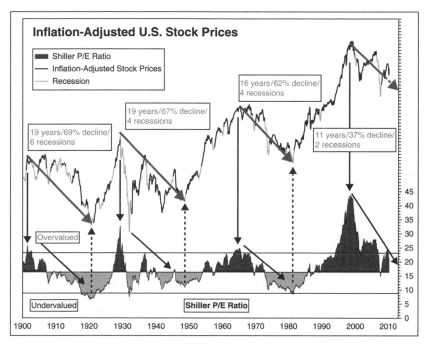

*Noted economist Robert Shiller calculated the price/earnings ratio based on the
average inflation-adjusted earnings from the previous 10 years, known as the
cyclically adjusted P/E ratio.
Source: http://www.econ.yale.edu/~shiller/data.htm; Pring Turner Capital Group

effects on earnings. This gauge of sentiment is continually moving
from a position of excessive optimism to one of pessimism and vice
versa. Why, at one time, are fearful investors willing to pay only $6.64
for $1 of earnings (i.e., at the 1982 secular bottom), while at another
time they are eager to pay $44.20 for that same $1 of earnings (i.e., at
the 2000 secular peak)? The answer lies in the extremes of confidence
or lack thereof seen only at major secular turning points. Obviously
investors are extremely confident at secular peaks. Otherwise why
on earth would they be willing to pay such astronomical valuations?

Similarly at secular lows they are so pessimistic that only fire sale prices will encourage them to buy stocks.

We have identified two extreme levels of sentiment—a Shiller P/E of 22.5 and above as a proxy for overoptimism and 7.5 and below for excessive despondency. You can see that over the past century and more the P/E has continually swung between these levels as highlighted by the arrows. Indeed, we can go further by saying that following each secular peak in overvaluation it has been necessary for the P/E to move back to the 7.5 zone before a new secular bull market could get under way. In other words, investors do not experience a shallow decline in their exuberant emotions and then go on to bid up prices in a wild manner. Rather this is a process in which emotions must go through a complete cycle including the despondent phase before a strong enough psychological condition can serve as a foundation for a new secular bull. Often it requires more than one move down to these basement levels. Table 3-1 summarizes the key turning points as well as other secular bear characteristics. Notice that at the beginning of the three twentieth-century secular bear markets the average P/E ratio is 27.3; in contrast the average at the end of these periods is 6.9.

Getting back to Chart 3-2, the absolute price level might have bottomed in 1932, but the P/E for the post–1929 bear market was

TABLE 3-1 Comparing Secular Bear Characteristics
It may take two or more business cycles for valuations to reach historic secular lows.

	Time Frame	Duration	No. of Recessions	Starting P/E	Finishing P/E	Decline (Inf.-Adj.)
1	**1901–1920**	19 Yrs 6 Months	6	25.2	5.1	−69%
2	1929–1949	19 Yrs 9 Months	4	32.6	9.1	−67%
3	1966–1982	16 Yrs 6 Months	4	24.1	6.6	−62%
	Average	18 Yrs 7 Months	4.7	27.3	6.9	−66%
4	2000–Dec. 2011	11 Yrs 4 Months	2	44.2	20.8	−37%

Source: http://www.econ.yale.edu/~shiller/data.htm; Pring Turner Capital Group

unable to really move away from the 7.5 area until 1949. That is one of the reasons why we classify this particular bear with that specific turning point.

The most recent observation at the start of 2012 registered a Shiller* P/E reading of just over 20. It is not quite as bad as it looks on the surface, since this is a rolling 10-year average based on annual earnings that will soon be rolling off some very low earnings numbers from the years 2002, 2003, and 2004. As these low numbers roll off and are replaced with more recent stronger earnings figures, the 10-year average P/E will automatically come down to the mid-teens even if earnings should go nowhere from here. Still, we may have traveled a long way from the 2000 historic overvaluation peak (P/E 44.2) but clearly much further price erosion or earnings gain would be required to reach truly undervalued levels (single digits) once again.

How Long Should We Expect the Secular Bear to Last?

In freely traded markets, the size of any particular mood change is often related to the level and extent of the emotion experienced during the previous trend. Thus it is normal for a four- to six-week rally to be followed by a two- to three-week correction or a cyclical bull market lasting two years to be followed by a bear lasting one year. The swing to the downside can be roughly proportionate, but since it takes longer to build than to tear down, bear moves normally take less time to unfold. The previous secular low in *absolute* prices developed in 1974, and the high was registered in 2000—a 26-year record secular bull run. That fact, together with the record levels of overvaluation at the peak in 2000, suggests that the current secular bear will be greater in magnitude and duration than the average.

---

*Noted economist Robert Shiller uses a proprietary 10-year average P/E ratio to smooth out the volatile business cycle effects on earnings. These data can be found at http://www.econ.yale.edu/~shiller/data.htm.

Previous post–1900 *inflation-adjusted* secular bear markets have lasted about 18 to 20 years. This was true for the 1901–1920 and 1966–1982 bears but only works for the post–1929 drop if we regard the period between 1932 and 1949 as a trading range. Indeed, in 1949 inflation-adjusted prices were not much above the 1932 low; nor was the P/E multiple. Let's also remember that the passage of a sufficient amount of time is a major requirement for a secular bear reversal. Time gives investors the ability to experience many difficult trials such as bear markets and recessions and sometimes even war. In total these setbacks have the effect of testing the stamina of investors and eventually pushing them into the totally discordant type of mood typically seen at secular lows. The 1929–1932 drop was the worst on record, but in a secular sense it was one of magnitude, not duration. Large generalized margin calls typically produce price lows. However, before prices can begin a sustainable bull market, a lot of base building and volatility are generally required. We think that is really what happened with the secular bear of the 1930–1940s when a giant (1929–1932) margin call was followed by 17 years of uncertainty and fear. Finally, enough time had lapsed to allow prices to begin a new secular bull in 1949.

Taking the year 2000 as our peak and even allowing the best (shortest) case, the 16-year bear period between 1966 and 1982 would project a low in 2016.

Now that you are in a better position to understand the importance of sufficient duration, please take a look at Chart 3-3, which shows the current bear overlaid on the average of its three predecessors.

In early 2012 the current bear had obviously progressed some way in terms of magnitude, but a projection based on the average duration of these and the current Japanese long-term bear (1990–20??) would suggest that a new secular bull is unlikely to emerge until at least two more (post–2008) business cycles have transpired.

CHART 3-3 Current Secular Bear Compared to the Average U.S. Experience Since 1900

More challenges lie ahead for stock investors, especially in inflation-adjusted terms.

Source: Pring Turner Capital Group

As discussed earlier, this combination of duration and inflation-adjusted price declines has historically ground away and eroded investor hope resulting in a total disgust with equities at the final low. It is not difficult to rationalize any number of economic or geopolitical problems that could push the market toward the eventual secular bear market bottom. However, our analysis is based on facts as characterized by the nature of previous bottoms rather than on opinion.

A simple approach that measures the stamina of investor psychology involves quantifying the number of recessions required to correct the previous bullish excesses. For reference purposes recessions are flagged in Chart 3-2 by the light highlights.

Prior secular bear trends have averaged between four and six recessions. Just compare that to the 1982–2000 secular bull market, which experienced just *one* recession in 1990. The reason why secular bears are so pregnant with economic contraction goes back to one of our previous points—one that concerns the structural excesses built up during the course of the previous secular bull. It is these structural headwinds that curtail the recovery part of business cycles that develop under the context of a secular bear. Structural headwinds have the effect of pushing the economy back into recession before it has had a chance to really get going again. Eventually, the excesses are worked off, and the new secular bull is born, but not before several meaningful contractions have taken place.

As of early 2012 we have experienced only two economic contractions during the course of the secular bear that began at the turn of the century. Even if we assume that the current secular bear will experience the best-case scenario of only four recessions, this leads us to the conclusion that U.S. equities in early 2012 are barely halfway through the secular bear cycle.

Our final point concerning duration is featured in Chart 3-3. The point also embraces some psychological aspects because the waves themselves essentially reflect the ebb and flow of investors' emotions. In short, the greater the number of waves and the larger their magnitude, the more substantial the psychological roller coaster is. At the end of many down waves, it's clear that the market has done a great job in promoting pessimism and desperation; both represent an excellent psychological foundation for a bull market.

The waves in the bottom panel of Chart 3-4 indicate price swings in excess of 25 percent. As you can see, the two previous secular cycles experienced seven such waves and the most recent 1966–1982 bear traced out five. This visual helps explain the fact that secular bear periods are deeply cyclical in nature as opposed to the secular bull periods which show much less stock volatility. For instance, the 1949–1966 secular bull market experienced no occurrences of a

CHART 3-4 Secular Bear Markets Are Deeply Cyclical Affairs

It is possible to build wealth in a secular bear market. One way is by taking advantage of business cycle swings.

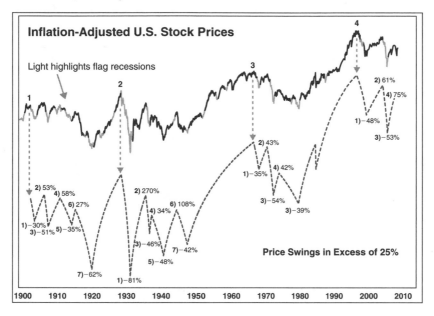

Source: Pring Turner Capital Group

25 percent inflation-adjusted market decline. In the 1982–2000 secular bull, only one such large decline occurred (during the 1987 crash), and that was relatively short and was followed by a new cyclical bull taking prices to new highs fairly quickly. The 1987 crash was not associated with a recession or even a serious economic slowdown. That came three years later in the form of the 1990 recession. In the current secular bear, three complete waves were registered between 2000 and 2009, and a fourth one got under way in March 2009. Again, when consideration is given to previous bear markets, more time and price swings appear likely.

Chart 3-5 offers a final approach to this idea of duration as it compares the current secular bear to its three predecessors. The target area has been flagged with the elliptical shading.

CHART 3-5 Comparing the Current Secular Bear to Its Predecessors
When will the current secular bear market finally reach bottom? Using history as a guide, generational low valuation levels and the start of a new secular bull market could begin in the 2016–2020 target area.

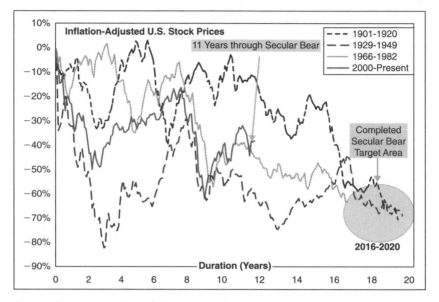

Source: Pring Turner Capital Group

We should not get too hung up on the average duration of previous U.S. bears because experience in Japan is far worse. Japanese equities started their secular bear market in 1989 and have so far outstripped the duration of any U.S. experience. The Japanese stock market has been under water for 22 years and shows little sign of regaining its old price highs. Keeping in mind that our current bear began with the most elevated Shiller P/E ratio in history, we would not be surprised if this one ends up being the longest secular bear in U.S. history.

The Role of Unstable Commodity Price Trends

So far we have considered the influence of psychology on secular equity trends, but there is another important aspect to consider, and that is the influence of unstable commodity prices. The long-term trend of commodity prices appears to have an enormous effect on the direction of the secular trend of inflation-adjusted stock prices. This relationship is demonstrated quite clearly in Chart 3-6. The series in the upper panel shows real stock prices since the mid-nineteenth century. The secular bear markets since then have been flagged with the dashed arrows. It is fairly evident that all of them, with the exception of the 1929–1932 experience, have been associated with a background of rising commodity prices. The relationship is not an exact tick by tick correlation, but the chart clearly demonstrates that a sustained trend of rising commodity prices sooner or later results in the demise of equities. The series we are using here is an index constructed from industrial raw materials (CRB Spot Raw Industrials). We like it because it consists of industrially traded

CHART 3-6 **Secular Trends in U.S. Equities Relative to Commodity Prices, 1850–2011**
Commodities are, in a secular bull market, historically a bad environment for stock prices. Secular bull markets for stocks occur when commodity prices are stable or falling.

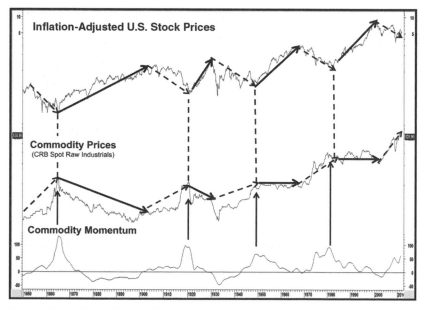

Source: Pring Turner Capital Group

commodities that are not influenced by the weather or speculative trading. Since this series has a history only going back to 1948, it has been spliced to previous wholesale commodity indexes prior to that date.

The one exception to this relationship, in the 1929–1932 period, was caused by instability of a different sort, where commodity prices experienced unusual volatility, but this time on the downside. After that, sharply rising commodity prices resulted in an extension of the secular bear. It is worth noting that the other two previous secular bears also experienced pockets of downside commodity turbulence. For example, the final drop in the 1900–1921 secular bear experienced an unusually sharp decline in commodity prices. Moreover, in the period between 1980 and 1982 the CRB Spot Raw Industrial Index fell by over 30 percent. Returning to Chart 3-6, we see that from 1949 until the mid–1960s commodities experienced a trading range, while equities enjoyed a secular bull market. The thick solid arrows show that *a sustained trend of falling or stable commodity prices is positive for equities* as all secular bulls developed under such an environment. This point is also underscored by the opening decade of the last century. It is labeled a secular bear, but real equity prices were initially quite stable as they were able to shrug off the gentle rise in commodities. Only when commodity prices accelerated to the upside a few years later did inflation-adjusted stock prices sell off sharply.

A useful approach for identifying a secular peak in commodity prices and usually a secular low in equities is to calculate a price oscillator or trend deviation measure. In this case the parameters used in Chart 3-6 are a 24-month (2-year) simple moving average divided by a 240-month (20-year) average.

The downward pointing arrows indicating reversals from an overextended position have offered four reliable signals in the last 150 years or so. The oscillator also peaked in 1975, but this proved to be a temporary respite for both the secular equity bear and the commodity bull markets. In addition the indicator reversed direction to the downside in 2008 but at early 2012 the long-term momentum trend for commodities by this measure was still rising and showing no sign of reversal. We suspect that this positive trend for commodities will stay in force for as long as the secular bear market for stocks remains in place. Later chapters will address how to take advantage of the continuing bull market in commodities, but for now we want to emphasize the importance of this intermarket relationship between the price of stocks and industrial raw materials.

Finally, the concepts discussed in this chapter do not represent a complete list of things you should be looking for at a secular turning point. In this respect some additional concepts are presented in Appendix A, so if you wish to explore these possibilities further, please refer to that section.

Where Is the Bottom?

Secular trends in equity prices are very much tied in with psychology, which itself is continually fluctuating between euphoria and extreme pessimism, just like the swinging of the pendulum of a clock. This psychological pendulum is much slower to reach its extremes, averaging something like 20 years per swing. Using the average of around 18 years of the three secular bears since 1900, the next swing would project to 2018. We are certainly not making such a prediction. However, at the bottom we might see a Shiller P/E in the single-digit area. Also, as discussed in detail in Appendix A, where we have added material for the investment enthusiast seeking more evidence, the dividend yield on the S&P 500 may approach around 6 percent, and the Tobin Q ratio, which is the market value of a company divided by the replacement value of the firm's assets, may hit an undervalued range of between 30 and 40. Please refer to the appendix for information on these valuation gauges and additional characteristics of secular turning points.

Generally speaking, the environment at a secular bear market low is one of total disgust with equities, where other investment categories are considered to be safer or to offer superior returns. The environment is also one in which it seems that equities will never regain their old highs. The combination of rampant investor pessimism and severe market undervaluation sets up the conditions for the start of a new secular bull market. The *key is to survive* the more difficult cyclical environment likely in the next decade as the secular bear market plays out, so you can fully partake in the secular bull market that will certainly follow.

KEY POINTS

1. Long-term trends are caused by extreme swings in psychology and between periods of stable and extreme commodity volatility.
2. Secular trends change at extreme valuation levels.
3. The current secular bear market could last until 2016–2022 or longer.
4. Be aware of the secular bull market in commodities and take advantage of it.
5. Investors must learn to capitalize on *cyclical* stock market opportunities and be prepared to protect capital in the cyclical declines.

IMPORTANT QUESTIONS FROM THE SMITHS

Each secular bull market has witnessed a major development that catapulted the economy higher. What will the next big thing be?

It is true that new secular bull markets have begun amidst the emergence of a new "big thing." In the late 1800s it was the railroads and the industrialization of the United States. In the 1920s it was the birth of the automobile industry and radio. After World War II, the rebuilding of the world and a higher standard of living for a new baby boom generation was key to growth, especially where consumer spending took off as the depression-era mentality finally wore off. In the 1980s and 1990s the adaptation of the personal computer for use in office workstations and the introduction of the Internet gave the economy an enormous productivity boost.

It is hard to say right now what the next "big thing" will be that will define the next secular bull market, should it begin in the year 2020 or so. Will it be in biotechnology and healthcare? Or perhaps a cheap new source of clean energy (natural gas from shale)? Or revolutionary developments in nanotechnology that dramatically boost productivity? Nobody can predict for sure, but one thing is likely: the new market leadership will not come from the prior leaders, in this case the commodity sector. Just as technology held the leadership position in the 1990s and thoroughly underperformed for years thereafter, an entirely new leadership theme will emerge in the 2020s. It will be interesting to see what the new development will be that helps launch the new secular bull era. Certainly it will pay to be very observant to find the clues that answer this question.

CHAPTER 4

INFLATION, INFLATION, INFLATION! THE SECULAR BULL MARKET IN COMMODITIES IS ALREADY WELL UNDER WAY

O ur retirement couple, the Smiths, like most Americans, are well aware that prices for ordinary items like food, healthcare, gasoline, and utilities have steadily climbed over the last decade and at an increasing rate. Never mind that the reported government inflation rate, the consumer price index (CPI), is "under control" according to Federal Reserve Chairman Ben Bernanke. Annual increases in the social security checks the Smiths receive each month are calculated based on this misleading and government manipulated gauge of inflation. In 2010 and 2011 there was no increase at all in their payments because the government said that there was virtually no inflation. At least that is according to its CPI numbers. The Smiths and the rest of us know better. Each and every day we are reminded of rising inflation as we head to a supermarket, hospital, pharmacy, restaurant, or gas station. It is important to understand that prices do not move up in a straight line. Even when the secular trend of inflation and commodity prices is up, business cycle contractions result in periodic declines. However, these are usually truncated and short-lived. Some items like college education and medical expenses never seem to go down, regardless of how weak the economy is.

So what is behind the steady increase in prices? What is in store for us in the next decade? Are there any investment opportunities that can be taken advantage of? Where are the risks if commodity prices continue to climb? What effect will inflation have on stocks and bonds? How can investors adapt? These are all serious questions. The answers are critically important because they can help you to survive and prosper in the next lost decade for stocks.

It is worthwhile to keep an eye on trends in commodity prices because they provide clues about the direction of the business cycle. First, commodity prices are sensitive to changes in economic supply/demand relationships, which means that they are often a reliable leading indicator of inflation. In addition, changes in commodity prices flag changes in the level of economic activity. For example, a few months prior to the onset of a recession, demand is high so manufacturers stock up on raw materials. As the recession unfolds, demand slows. In turn, this leads to an excess of supply because inventory levels become bloated relative to the prevailing level of sales. Naturally when supplies are excessive and demand falls, so do prices, usually with a vengeance. Consequently, advances and declines in commodity prices can be used as one indicator for measuring economic health. To some extent we have to be a bit careful because the United States was by far the most dominant economic power for most of the twentieth century. However, in the decade prior to 2010, its share of global GDP sank from 40 percent to the mid-twenties. The United States is still the largest economy but by an ever-shrinking margin. As a result the U.S. influence on commodity price levels is less than it was. You can appreciate this fact by viewing Chart 4-1, which compares the fortunes of a U.S.-based commodity index (CRB Spot Raw Industrials) to the global economy. The shaded areas demonstrate that when global business activity is shrinking, commodity prices in the U.S. suffer and vice versa.

CHART 4-1 CRB Spot Raw Industrials Versus Global Economic Momentum
Commodity prices are sensitive to the global economy and are a leading indicator of inflation.

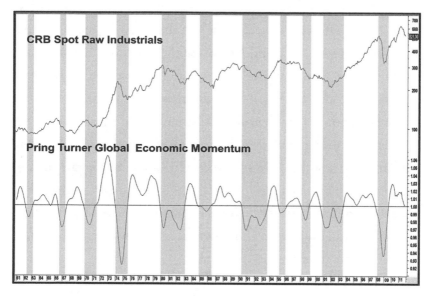

Note: Shaded areas represent global economic slowdowns, which are weak periods for commodity prices.
Source: Pring Turner Capital Group

We think of rising commodity prices as inflationary, but when they suck out some of the purchasing power from consumers, they have a deflationary effect. Just ask American drivers on a tight budget about the importance of gas prices in the United States rising from just above $1.50 a gallon in 2008 to as high as $4 in 2012, not to mention the rise in heating oil if they choose to stay warm at home. For folks on a fixed income or in retirement like the Smiths, it is an even greater challenge.

Food price inflation is not as important for the developed world as it is for emerging market countries where the proportion of income spent on food is far greater. But rising food prices in the United States do take an additional toll on precious retirement income. Healthcare costs are also rising faster than the inflation rate. Although medical care is better than it has ever been, for the Smiths costs are at record levels.

What is causing commodity prices to rise so dramatically? One would think that the relatively weak U.S., European, and Japanese economies would keep a lid on prices since demand from these slow-growth economies is so low. This is where the emerging markets come into play—Brazil, India, and China are the big three, but there are plenty of other growth stories in Asia, Latin America, Africa, Eastern Europe, and the Middle East. The common traits among these fast-growing economies are their relatively young and upwardly mobile populations, strong sovereign balance sheets, and a rapidly rising standard of living that creates a voracious appetite for raw materials. In the past these nations exported more commodities than they imported from the rest of the world. Now a lot of them must import oil, copper, iron ore, grains, and other essential raw materials to meet accelerating internal consumer demand.

Making matters worse was the long-term disinvestment in new raw material supplies during the last secular bear market for commodities. The 20-year period from 1980 to 2000 followed the last boom period for commodities in the 1970s. That boom led to an extended period of ample supplies and resulting net shrinkage in new mining, exploration, and farming projects worldwide. Some of you might remember oil prices falling from $40 a barrel in 1981 to $10 a barrel in the 1990s. With prices falling for many commodity markets, what was the incentive to explore and develop new projects? By the year 2000 demand caught up and overcame supply which has translated into higher prices and the beginning of a new secular bull market for commodities. Since it takes a very long time to plan, permit, finance, build, and finally produce new copper, gold, oil, or even farming projects, this commodity rally dating from the start of the century has plenty of time before once again supply overtakes demand. In our mind, this may not happen until 2016–2022 or so, which corresponds nicely with the continuing secular bear market for stocks time frame we envision. That is not to say that we will not experience business cycle–associated commodity price declines along the way. Indeed we have already experienced two such setbacks—one in 2008 and one that started in 2011. At the start of 2012 though, the secular uptrend is still intact. Until we see evidence to the contrary, our assumption is that it will continue. Also, the historical long-term inverse correlation between inflation-adjusted equities and commodities remains in force. The more things change, the more they stay the same.

Another important reason we expect the commodity boom to continue relates to the U.S. and other developed countries' monetary policy decisions. Especially in the aftermath of the global financial crisis in 2008–2009, central banks around the globe are pursuing a policy of rapid monetary stimulus (printing money), and in the long run this can only lead to weaker currencies. Lower currency values translate into higher prices for commodities. Imagine the playground teeter-totter; on one side place hard assets (real stuff you can touch), and on the other side place paper assets (currencies). (See Figure 4-1.) As currency values decline, hard asset values appreciate and vice versa. No better example can be found than by looking at the U.S. dollar relative to the price of gold—the ultimate hard versus paper asset relationship.

It is a good idea to prepare for the next potential crisis out there—accelerating inflation—as the commodity secular bull continues. Obviously we do not have a crystal ball, so we cannot pinpoint precisely when that will happen. Two key conflicting issues in this regard are a potential inflationary explosion in the monetary base and the debilitating effects of a deflationary structural debt overhang. This relationship gets a bit complicated but cannot be ignored. We cover it in Appendix B for those who wish to drill down on these important monetary and structural issues.

FIGURE 4-1 Dollar versus Gold: The Ultimate Hard Versus Paper Asset Relationship

As currency values decline, hard asset values appreciate and vice versa.

Inflation: The Stealth Tax on Portfolios

In Chapter 3 we explained that secular trends in equity prices are caused by generational swings in psychology as well as unusual instability in commodity prices. Now it is time to more closely examine the other important driver—the long-term volatility in commodity markets. More broadly based measurements of inflation such as the CPI are important, but we focus on industrial commodity prices. These prices have a tendency to lead the CPI, are less subject to manipulation, and are far more sensitive to cyclical and secular swings.

Inflation is a stealth tax on wealth that slowly eats away at the purchasing power of your investments. You will get taxed on your gains, but the IRS does not give you a tax credit for purchasing power lost to inflation. Take our friends the Smiths. If they manage to grow their portfolio from, say, $1 million to $1.4 million over a five-year period (7 percent annual return), they must pay capital gains tax on those profits when they sell. However, if the CPI increases by a modest 2.5 percent per annum, they will actually lose about 13 percent in purchasing power over those five years. Look at it this way. After paying the 15 percent capital gains tax, they will be left with $1,340,000 in cash. However, the purchasing value of that cash will be degraded by a further 13 percent through inflation. That combination will bring their real (tax and inflation-adjusted) nest egg to less than $1,185,000. They are still above their starting level, not by the illusionary 40 percent, but by a mere 18.5 percent in *real* terms.

It gets worse. Financial assets represent savings for future purchases. Failure to increase their inflation-adjusted value results in a loss of purchasing power and a downgrade in lifestyle. If you are retiring in your mid-sixties with an adequate but not overly generous nest egg, you will need to grow that asset base by more than the rate of inflation to maintain your lifestyle. Anyone digging into capital and unable to survive off the income alone will face an even more serious problem as time goes by. In a secular bull where mistakes are quickly bailed out, this is still a challenge, but in a secular bear the difficulties are overwhelming. When retirees regularly withdraw funds from their account for living expenses, preservation of capital becomes especially critical. Consequently, it is virtually impossible for retirees to maintain their standard of living if their nest egg endures significant market losses as in the recent lost decade. It will be the case again with a buy-and-hold strategy in any future secular bear market.

Now that we have established that inflation reduces the spending power of savings over time, let us address the reality that secular trends in equities are affected by significant changes in inflationary threats. To justify our secular bear argument for equities, we make a case for excessive commodity inflation. Our first task is to establish the link between secular equity trends and commodity prices.

The second is to examine the direction of the current commodity price trend and forecast how long it might extend. For now, we want to focus on commodity price inflation and its effect on investor portfolios. The remainder of this chapter covers our long-term stock, bond, and commodity themes and should help you better understand our outlook for the next decade.

Characteristics of Secular Commodity Trends

Chart 4-2 features U.S. commodity prices since 1840 with arrows flagging the secular trends. Most of them rise or fall for extended periods of time. However, since the inception of the Federal Reserve, two of the three secular bear markets have really been multiyear trading ranges.

CHART 4-2 Characteristics of Secular Commodity Trends
The average secular bull market for commodities lasts 19 years. The current secular bull began in 2002 and is still quite young in 2012 by historical standards.

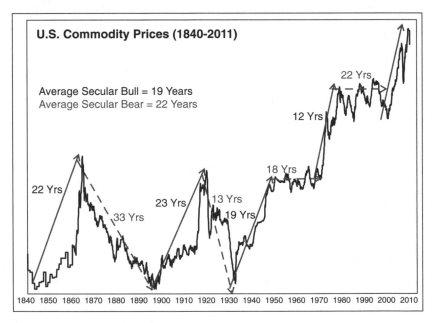

Source: Pring Turner Capital Group

This demonstrates the very low tolerance monetary authorities have for deflationary effects of falling prices. Given the chance, you can bet that monetary authorities will always err on the side of inflation.

The numbers against the arrows show the length of these secular price movements, secular bulls lasting on average for 19 years and secular bears for 22.

The current commodity secular bull move began in 2002, so at the start of 2012 it was quite young by historical standards. If it were to last the average secular bull duration, this would imply a peak sometime near 2020. That general time frame fits in nicely, give or take a year or two, with the approximate average duration of previous U.S. secular equity bears.

The Influence of Commodity Price Trends
on Secular Trends in Equities

Now let us reexamine the relationship between stocks and commodities that was introduced in an earlier chapter. To recap, secular *bear* markets for stocks are historically associated with secular *bull* markets for commodities. By way of rationalization, a period of rising raw material prices might cut into corporate profit margins and make life more treacherous for stock investors. Consequently, as inflation heats up, investors become less inclined to buy stocks. This results in their P/E ratios steadily declining with each inflationary wave. In addition, rising commodity prices also discourage investors from owning bonds because inflation eats up their purchasing power. At some point investors figure that it is worth the risk of owning bonds, but not until interest rates move sufficiently high as a means of compensation for the loss of purchasing power. Since stocks and bonds are competitive asset classes, the yield on stocks also has to go up, either in the form of higher dividends or lower prices or both.

Chart 4-3 features a ratio between stocks and commodities. As the ratio moves higher, stocks are outperforming commodities and vice versa. The shaded areas represent secular equity bear markets.

Remember that for long periods of time stocks, which are financial assets (paper), tend to move teeter-totter fashion in the opposite direction to commodities (hard assets). However, there can be no mistaking the fact that the vast majority of the time, when equities are in a secular bear market, they are being outperformed by commodities. Also included in the chart is the 96-month or 8-year moving average of the ratio. When the ratio is above its moving average, this typically signals a major equity bull market. On the other hand, when the ratio slips below its moving average, this usually happens in

CHART 4-3 **Stock Prices Relative to Commodities**
As the stock/commodity ratio moves higher, stocks are outperforming commodities. As the ratio moves lower, commodities outperform stocks, as is the case since 2000. The three previous secular bull markets for stocks were all preceded by a rally in this ratio.

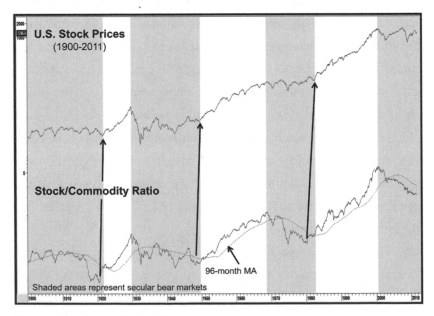

Source: Pring Turner Capital Group

a secular bear market scenario. Since 1950 we have seen only one false crossover, where the signal did not hold for an extended period, and that was in 1970—not bad for a 60-year record. As you can see, the stock/commodity series fell below its moving average in the opening year of the decade and has been there ever since. Its next upside crossover will probably offer a timely and accurate signal that a new equity secular bull market is underway. One other key observation is that the three previous secular bulls were all preceded by a serious rally in this ratio. They have been flagged with the rightward pointing arrows in Chart 4-3.

Any momentum series assumes in its calculation that prices are undergoing a cycle of a specific length. If that cycle diverges significantly from that time span, reversals in such velocity measures are likely to be unduly late or, on occasion, premature. This is why we demand that such signals be confirmed by a reaction from in the price they might be monitoring. In other words, if a smoothed momentum series reverses direction, we want to make sure that the price is responding to it. Responses could take the form of a moving average violation, the penetration of a trendline, and so on. In Chart 4-3 bullish confirmation is given when the price crosses above its 96-month moving average. This is when the plot is experiencing a light highlight. Unfortunately we are unable to reproduce colors in the book. However, where appropriate, the charts on the website are in color, and for this one red highlights develop when both technical measures are negative and black when they are in conflict. Most of these signals have been reasonably accurate, but the numerous black highlights (on the website chart) remind us that the system is far from perfect.

At the start of 2012 the oscillator was rising but was not particularly overextended. Based on previous behavior, where reversals took place from a much higher level, the secular trend dating from 2002 could have the potential to extend well into the second decade of the century. A lot will depend on how the market handles the cyclical bear market that began in early 2011. The signal we would look for to trigger a reversal in the secular uptrend would be a break below the two converging trendlines and the 96-month moving average. At the start of 2012 the CRB Spot Raw Industrial Index was slightly above 500, and the lower of these support zones stood at around 370. This means there was considerable leeway on the downside before a secular reversal signal would be triggered. Data updates can be obtained at http://www.crbtrader.com/crbindex/crbdata.asp.

Identifying Reversals in the Secular Trend

One problem with identifying secular trends and understanding their characteristics is that there are very few data points. Chart 3-3 for example, features the CRB Spot Raw Industrials. The history of this index goes back only to 1948, so it has been spliced to other historical data series in order to give us a longer time perspective.

During the last 200 years or so, there have been nine commodity secular bull and bear markets as flagged by the arrows. We are now in the tenth. Not all secular trends experience the same characteristics. For example, the mid- to late-nineteenth-century bear was a slow drawn-out decline. The 1920–1933 trend experienced two sharp down waves compared to the trading range characteristics of the 1980–2000 period. These differing patterns make consistent and timely identification of secular trend reversals a somewhat difficult task. One technique is to smooth the data with a very long-term moving average so that the underlying trend can be better reflected. Unfortunately, even the best time spans are subject to numerous whipsaw or false crossovers resulting from the volatility of the data and are often unduly late in triggering signals. For this reason the application of smoothed long-term momentum indicators seems to offer a more reliable signal.

CHART 4-4 U.S. Commodity Prices and a Long-Term Momentum Indicator
Long-term price momentum points to continued commodity price gains and shows
no sign of imminent reversal.

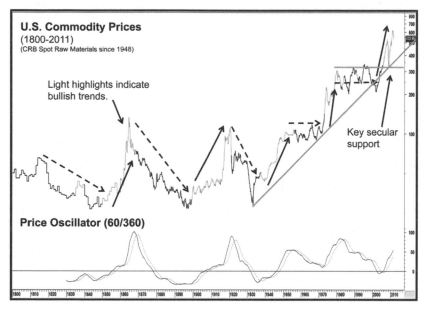

Source: Pring Turner Capital Group

An example is shown in Chart 4-4, where a 360-month (30-year
moving average) has been divided by a 60-month (5-year) period.

These may seem like unduly long time spans, but remember that
we are dealing with trends that encompass many individual business
cycles, and they require really long-term smoothing. Secular momentum buy and sell signals are triggered when the oscillator crosses
above and below its 48-month (4-year) moving average, represented
by the dashed line. As long as this momentum series is in a rising
trend, it is assumed that the secular trend is positive and vice versa.
Do not forget that the key charts in this book are periodically updated
on our website at www.pringturner.com as are our conclusions resulting from any changes that might take place.

Investment Opportunities in Inflation-Sensitive Assets

The bad news is that the stock market is probably in for rough sledding for the bulk of another decade. The good news is that there is a secular bull market in real assets going on, and it is not too late to participate. Yes, there will be cyclical corrections along the way, like the 2008–2009 commodity slide and the cyclical decline that started in 2011. These could be quite painful.

However, if you are observant and fortunate enough to spot a new cyclical commodity bull market as the secular uptrend resumes, there are a host of rewarding vehicles. Much of the fundamental reason for their continued outperformance lies in the outlook for economic growth in the emerging economies. Their young and growing middle class continues to voraciously gobble up important natural resources. Energy, metals, and agricultural products will continue to see higher demand as standards of living accelerate in the fastest growing parts of the world. It will be a long while before supply catches up to demand. We suspect that it may very well take us into the latter part of this decade to finally come into balance.

Some examples of inflation-sensitive opportunities are: natural resource stocks, commodities, and resource-based countries like Brazil, Canada, and Australia. These showed impressive gains in the first decade of the secular equity bear (secular commodity bull). We fully expect their leadership attributes to extend in the decade ahead, so here are a few ideas to help you participate in these resource-based sectors.

Assets that historically perform well when commodity prices rise are called *inflation hedges* because that is what they do—they offer a hedge against inflation. For example, inflation tends to become more troublesome when the U.S. dollar is weak. One tactic could include using international bonds denominated in a currency of a leading natural resource–based country, such as Canada or Australia. An obvious choice would be exposure to inflation beneficiaries such as energy, metals, mining, agricultural, and forest products companies. Many equity investments within these groups provide strong free cash flows and growing dividend streams that provide healthy income and stability to an investor's nest egg. Another possibility is the purchase of natural resource ETNs (exchange-traded notes) specializing in specific commodities, sectors, or broadly based commodity indexes. A word of caution: since many of these ETN vehicles are based on futures contracts, it is important to check out their tax implications for your portfolio before buying since most produce a K–1 tax form. Precious metals (gold, silver, platinum) are another obvious choice. Investors can also look for yield in resource-based investment trusts both in the United States and Canada, where generous income returns are typically offered with the growth kicker of ownership of real assets.

What we have witnessed over the last decade is a steady shift of investment from "paper" assets (like currencies) to "real" assets (like precious metals). Recall Figure 4-1 that shows the two opposing asset classes on a symbolic teeter-totter and represents the flow from one side of the investment ledger to the other. These shifts have been alternating in a fairly consistent manner within our secular observations described in the earlier part of the book. In other words, once a trend gets started, it can take a couple of decades to fully play out, and so far we are only halfway along this path. There is a very good possibility that the commodity theme will end up in a parabolic move that really gathers broad investor enthusiasm, much as it did in the late 1970s, or even as the tech bubble gained momentum in the late 1990s. That will certainly serve as a warning sign to take caution and, equally important, as a sign that the secular bear market for stocks is nearing its ending phase. Only after the commodity bull market ends can a new secular bull market for stocks (paper assets) get started again. The new secular bull market for stocks will begin with completely new leadership that will most certainly not include the resource-based sectors. That's something to think about as we get closer to 2020. For now, it still makes sense to understand the secular bull commodity theme and take advantage of it.

Combining these inflation-sensitive investments will enable investors to take advantage of the continued commodity boom and help retirees like the Smiths temper the effects of accelerating inflation rates. The Smiths do not have to be victims of inflation but can prosper during an inflationary spiral.

KEY POINTS

1. As long as commodities are in a secular uptrend, stocks will likely be in a secular bear market.
2. Hard assets (commodities, gold, etc.) tend to move inversely to paper assets.
3. Protecting purchasing power will be an increasingly important and difficult task as the commodity theme plays out.
4. Take advantage of opportunities in inflation-sensitive assets that are in secular uptrends.

IMPORTANT QUESTIONS FROM THE SMITHS

Some commentators are saying that the Fed is printing too much money through its policy of quantitative easing and that this is going to lead to inflation. However, the next time we tune in someone else reminds us that the United States is borrowing so much money that it is eventually going to go broke and that this is going to lead to deflation. What do you think?

The U.S. bond market has experienced a 31-year trend of declining yields, and we believe that this will soon change. If you look at previous turning points, bond yields have not usually reversed on a dime but have experienced extended trading ranges prior to moving up. We think this is also possible this time around. If it is, it would mean several years of sideways volatility as the deflationary effects of a partial unwinding of government excesses both here and in Europe are felt. We also think that the Fed has put too much money into the system and that eventually this liquidity will move from the banking system into goods and services, resulting in inflation. We will do our best to keep you up to date with our latest views at www.pringturner.com. There you will find the occasional chart, article, and quarterly client newsletters, all of which are freely available to the public.

CHAPTER 5

LOOKING OUT FOR A POTENTIAL CHANGE TO THE UPSIDE FOR INTEREST RATES

After reading our case for a continued secular bull market in commodities and higher inflation in Chapter 4, the Smiths are probably wondering about the implications for their bond investments. Before we launch into a discussion on the long-term interest-rate trend change, a brief and basic primer of terms is useful. Often, inexperienced investors get lost in the jargon common to the investment world. The terms *yield* and *interest rates* are usually used interchangeably in bond discussions. There is a difference however. *Interest rate* is the return originally given to a debt instrument (bond or note) and once issued is generally fixed for the life of the debt instrument. This is often referred to as the "coupon rate." The original interest rate is expressed as a percent of the principal amount of the bond. Once the bond trades in the marketplace, the price will fluctuate based on changes in general market conditions, credit rating changes, and interest-rate changes. *This is the yield.* But the world changes, and the value of the bond changes as interest rates change. So how does an existing or previously issued bond compete when new ones come to the marketplace at different interest rates? Its price and yield must

FIGURE 5-1 Bond Price to Yield Teeter-Totter
Bond prices go down as interest rates go up.

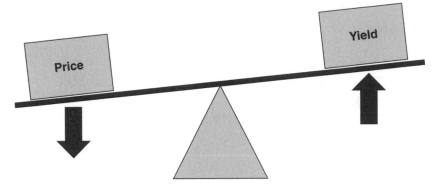

Source: Pring Turner Capital Group

adjust. The easiest way to visualize this process is to picture a teeter-totter. Price is balanced at one end of the teeter-totter, and yield is at the other (Figure 5-1).

For example, if current market yields move up, the price of the bond will decline. When market yields drop, the price of the bond will rise. Importantly, the longer to the maturity, the bigger the price swings in bond prices. Thus long-term bonds have greater price volatility than shorter-term bonds. When we talk about the secular trend in prices or yields, keep in mind the teeter-totter diagram because it helps make the material easier to understand.

So what is the secular outlook for bonds, and how will it affect the Smiths' portfolio? The secular bear market in stocks has benefited bondholders as many frustrated investors have fled to the "safe haven" of bonds. Interest rates continued to fall (bond prices continue to rise) from the high levels seen in 1981. This secular bull market has truly been a once in a lifetime event. Hindsight is 20/20, and looking back 30 years, U.S. government bonds yielding 15 percent were an incredible opportunity in 1981. However, at that time few people were inclined to take advantage of it. Instead, investors were afraid of falling bond prices and the inflation bogeyman that had ravaged bond portfolios *the prior 40 years!* Money market funds paid almost the same rate of return as long-term bonds but with daily liquidity and no principal risk, so why would anyone want to invest in bonds? As rates moved higher and higher, money fund yields tracked right along, keeping investor returns in line with the trend. We were managing portfolios at the time and have vivid memories of investor attitudes. The argument went something like this, "Why buy a bond, and take the risk of further losses if rates keep marching higher?" Tough for advisors to argue that point since bonds, on and off, had been losing money in client portfolios the prior 40 years. To help cope, brokers filled their trading days near year-end by providing an annual service called "tax-loss harvesting" to their beleaguered bond clients. By swapping an old bond at a loss into new bonds, clients could realize their capital tax loss, thereby reducing their tax liability. In essence, the strategy turned a paper loss into a real one. The extra portfolio activity surely helped bolster brokers' commissions, making it a favored time of year for them, and it made the clients' tax preparers happy too. Unfortunately for the client, each year their bond portfolio values were painfully eroded.

The annual bond tax-swap ritual is a thing of the past because it has not been needed for some time. Regrettably, we think bond investors will have to refamiliarize themselves with the old tax-loss harvesting technique during the course of this next decade. If a new secular bear market for bonds gets underway, it will be a real game-changer. As a first step let's take a glance at U.S. government bond yields since 1860 because it will help us to identify long-term secular trend changes. The series plotted in Chart 5-1 is the U.S. government 30-year constant maturity (TYX) spliced to a 20-year series prior to 1994.

It is fairly evident that trends in bond yields are much better-behaved than their volatile commodity counterparts; this is beneficial to investors because it makes secular reversals relatively easier

CHART 5-1 The Secular Trends in U.S. Government Bond Yields, 1870–2011
U.S. government bond yields have experienced a secular downtrend (bull market for bond prices) since 1981 (31 years). A potential secular turning point could be close at hand.

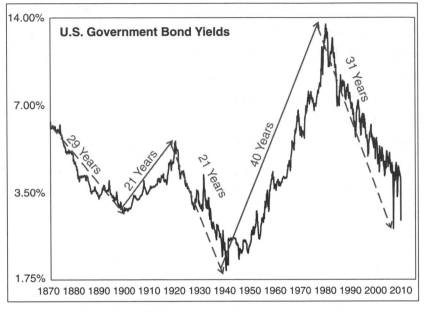

Source: Pring Turner Capital Group

to identify. The arrows show the five secular trends since 1870. The two completed bear markets for bond prices (bull markets in yields) averaged 30 years, and the bull markets for bond prices (bear markets in yields) averaged 25 years. U.S. bond yields have been in a secular downtrend (bull market for bond prices) since 1981 or for about 31 years at the start of 2012. In terms of time served, this favorable bond trend is long in the tooth, which makes us believe that a potential turning point could be close at hand.

For the Smiths, who are in their early seventies, the 31-year secular decline in yields means that they have enjoyed a wonderful bull market in bonds during just about their entire investment lifetime. As interest rates steadily declined with each business cycle to lower and lower levels, bond prices appreciated. Any cyclical rise in yields was temporary and followed by successive new low-yield levels. Mortgage refinancing became a popular ritual for them and every other U.S. homeowner wishing to reduce monthly mortgage payments along the way. Their bond investments, whether in individual holdings with a specific maturity date or funds, produced steady income as well as capital growth as bond prices climbed. It was a one-way street to happy returns. Indeed, had the Smiths been exclusively exposed to bonds, during the last decade they would have completely missed two devastating bear markets in equities.

The point we are making is that the Smiths have spent a majority of their investment horizon in an environment of declining interest rates. Like every other investor of their time, they have known nothing else. Rising bond prices have become expected. High-quality bond instruments have earned the reputation of being virtually risk-free investments. Complacency and a false sense of security have set in, and this is a dangerous investment condition because it means that few, if any, are prepared for a reversal. History, though, tells a different story. The facts are that these secular swings do not last forever. Today conditions are ripe for a reversal to the upside for yields. The actual sting of higher and higher interest rates and a secular bear market with lower and lower bond prices has *never* been felt by most investors. Consequently, many are ill-prepared to face the challenges, and it is not likely that they will be able to adjust expectations when the very long-term trend changes.

The Implications for Investors of a Rising Secular Interest-Rate Trend

Between 2000 and 2011 bonds performed especially well in comparison to stocks as the secular bear market unfolded. Portfolios including a combination of stocks and bonds over the last 10 years witnessed poor equity performance but excellent bond returns. This combination generated positive returns despite volatile and poor overall stock performance. However, if a secular advance in yields gets underway, long-term bonds will decline in price and will no longer be a safe haven. Indeed, the next decade could end up being *a lost decade for both stock and bond investors,* a lethal combination investors have not had to experience since the 1960s and 1970s. Fortunately we developed the necessary tools that allowed us to survive and prosper in the 1970s, and we share them with you in the chapters ahead.

The various yield assumptions in Figure 5-2 help to emphasize that an unexpected advance in yields would be quite damaging to bond investors. For example, the rate on a 20-year government bond might rise from the (2.75 percent) level prevailing at the start of 2012

FIGURE 5-2 Higher Interest Rates Subject Bondholders to Principal Loss
Bond investors are subject to substantial principal loss as interest rates move higher.

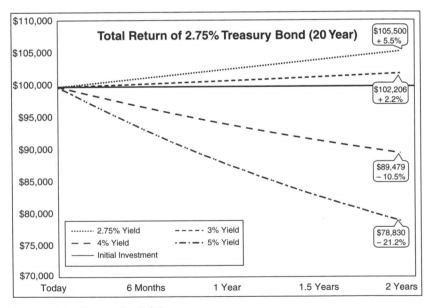

Source: Pring Turner Capital Group

to just 5 percent over the next two years. If this happens, an original $100,000 investment including interest would fall to $78,830 for a 21.2 percent loss.

Consider the massacre bond investors will suffer over a 10-, 20-, or 30-year secular bear market in bonds, as happened in the 1960s and 1970s. Today's paltry coupon income provides little protection to offset price losses with even a small increase in interest rates. When secular declines in interest rates are experienced, investors' future expectations are influenced because they become accustomed to the lower levels. It is easy to see why. If rates trade in the 3 to 4 percent range for several years, that level becomes the standard. It then becomes extremely difficult to imagine rates rising, even to their historical average of around 6 percent—the result would be a bloodbath of epic proportions.

The previous example showed a 20-year bond with a 2.75 percent coupon losing over 20 percent with just a modest interest-rate move to 5 percent in two years. Do you think that this is unlikely to happen? Please keep in mind that when 20-year yields were north of 15 percent in October 1981, the 10 percent level was unthinkably low. Fast-forward to May 1983 (just 19 months later) when rates actually were hovering around that "unthinkably" low level.

Why are we convinced that rates will rise in the coming decade? For that we need to talk about the principal driver of bond yields—the inflation rate. Inflation is important because investors demand a higher level of compensation when it is eating away at the purchasing power of their money. Bond investors generally require two components of return from their fixed income investments. The first is a risk premium. Mortgage companies, for example, will charge a higher rate to individuals with a low credit score than to those with a high one. Bond investors are no different. The second component, the inflation premium, is even more important to investors. This is because bond investors demand a full return not only on their principal but on the purchasing power of their principal. They are keenly aware of inflation risks and require returns that are above the inflation rate.

Thus, all this means that over time, there is a strong correlation between the trend of commodities, inflation, and bond yields. In fact commodity prices are a consistent leading indicator of bond yields. You are probably wondering why it works this way. In the early stages of a recovery, when the demand for inventories picks up, the balance between the demand and supply of commodities moves in favor of the demand side, so prices rise. Bond market participants notice that commodity prices are rising and anticipate that inflation is going to intensify. They start selling fixed income investments that struggle during inflationary environments; this pushes up yields. We cover the relationship between interest rates and inflation in greater detail when we drill down deeper into the business cycle in Chapter 6. For now, it is important to understand that higher inflation (commodity prices) leads to higher interest rates.

We can take this a step further by saying that commodity prices also have a strong tendency to lead yields at *secular* turning points. If the current secular trend for commodities is a rising one, bond yields ought to be moving in the same direction. Unfortunately, if interest rates are rising, bond prices are falling. With bonds declining in price and inflation eating away at their principal, investors face a double headwind. During the first decade of the current secular bear market in stocks, this was not a problem. Indeed, as explained earlier, bonds continued to rise during this time period and proved to be a safe haven for equity investors. Consequently, if the inflation scenario comes to pass, both stock and bond investors will find themselves under pressure, leaving commodities and inflation-sensitive equities as the only promising long-term games in town.

Identifying Secular Reversals in the Credit Markets

Throughout history U.S. bond yields have alternated between secular bull and bear trends just like stocks and commodities. History in this case goes back to the mid-nineteenth century. Since the financial crash of 2008, economists have debated whether the fiscal stimulus and extraordinary easy monetary policy (quantitative easing, QE I and II) would lead to a significant inflationary wave or whether the system would fall into a liquidity trap. A liquidity trap as defined in Keynesian economics develops when easy monetary policies are unable to stimulate an economy, either through lowering interest rates or increasing the money supply, thereby resulting in deflation. This is known as "pushing on a string." Either way this would extend the secular bear market in equities. However, a liquidity trap would be bullish for high-quality bonds since it would imply cheaper commodities and weaker economic growth. Our objective here is not to dwell on the economic arguments, but rather to examine the secular trends of commodities, bonds, and their intermarket relationship to see what clues the markets themselves may be giving about the inflation/deflation outlook. One technique we use to identify secular trend reversals in interest rates is some really basic trend analysis, as shown in Chart 5-2.

At this point it makes sense to make a few observations on trendline construction so that their characteristics can be appreciated. When we draw trendlines, our objective is to replicate the underlying trend. The more times a line has been touched or approached, the better it is as a reflector of the underlying trend. In addition, the longer the line, the bigger the trend being monitored and the more significant the eventual penetration. As you can see in the chart, this jagged indicator lends itself very nicely to trendline construction. When a meaningful long-term line has been penetrated, we get the first part of a two-part signal that the secular trend has reversed.

CHART 5-2 U.S. Government Bond Yields and Long-Term Momentum
At the start of 2012, bond yields and long-term momentum are at low levels and
the secular downtrend in yields is still intact. However, a trend reversal may not be
far away.

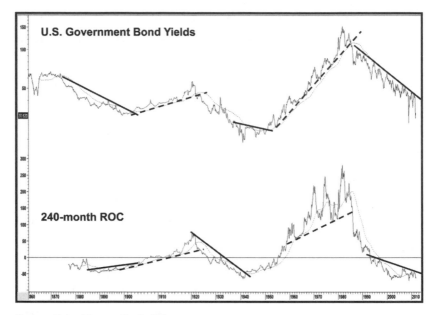

Source: Pring Turner Capital Group

The idea with the rate of change (ROC) indicator in the bottom half of Chart 5-2 is to identify long-term swings in the cyclical
rhythms. The second part of the signal comes when the yield itself
confirms the momentum penetration with a trendline violation of its
own. You can see from the chart how this very simple approach has
resulted in four excellent secular reversal signals. Not all long-term
trends have a convenient setup such as this, but in the second decade
of this century we are most fortunate in this respect. This is because
it is possible to construct a really meaningful down trendline for the
yield that started in the early 1980s. We also see a nice trendline on the
ROC indicator. Again at the start of 2012 both series remain intact,
indicating that the secular downtrend in yields or the secular uptrend
in bond prices remains alive and well.

There is one more useful signal triggering mechanism, and that is where we relate a 9-month exponential moving average (EMA) of the yield to its 96-month (8-year) exponential moving average. An exponential series is basically the same as a simple moving average except that its construction weights nearby observations more heavily so it turns quicker. Bearish periods, when the shorter-term EMA is below its longer-term counterpart, are represented in Chart 5-3 by the dark highlight for the yield.

Light highlights signal when the model is bullish for yields. To be sure, this approach has experienced some whipsaws or false signals in the last 150 years, such as the false upside breaks in 1890s and 1930s. However, this relationship has been extremely well-behaved in the several decades preceding 2012; the last false signal

CHART 5-3 U.S. Government Bond Yields and a Secular Trend Indicator
A reversal in this secular trend indicator has not yet been signaled, but it would indicate a secular trend change for bonds from good to bad.

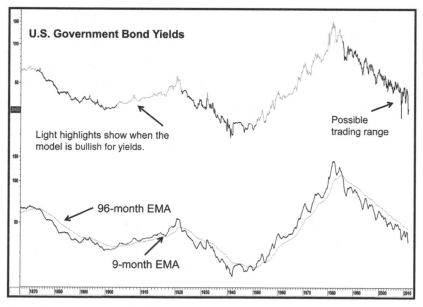

Source: Pring Turner Capital Group

81

was seen in the 1950s. It has certainly been the case since the early 1980s that the 9-month EMA has traded below the 96-month EMA on a consistent basis. You can probably see this more clearly from the lower panel in the chart, which features both averages. Many attempts have been made at an upside crossover, but each attempt has failed. This consistent inability to trigger a reversal increases the significance of the 96-month EMA as a dynamic resistance area. What this means is that when a positive crossover does finally materialize, it is likely to represent an accurate signal that the secular downtrend has reversed. When the (EMA/trendline) zone is finally cracked, we believe it will signal an end to the current secular downtrend in yields (bull market for bond prices). At the start of 2012 the trendline and moving average were around 4.4 percent for the 30-year bond.

We have emphasized the fact that bond yields historically have moved in long-term trends, both up and down, which is the case the vast majority of the time. However, if you study Chart 5-3 closely, you will see that yields often experience extended trading ranges at secular lows prior to the uptrend getting under way. This was true, for example, between 1886 and 1906 and more recently for the 11 years between 1939 and 1951. In other words, if the massive monetary stimulation following the 2007–2008 recession fails to immediately translate into inflation because of the debt overhang problem discussed earlier, we could well be in for a bout of deflation and stable rates at lower levels prior to the next secular upswing of inflation.

Our feeling is that if a deflationary outcome does develop as the second decade in the century unfolds, it will be temporary and will eventually give way to an inflationary one as has always been the case in the past.

Commodities Lead Bond Yields at Secular Lows

The vast majority of the time the secular trends of commodity prices and bond yields move in the same direction. Therefore, as a general rule if commodity prices are in a sustainable uptrend, bond yields will be in one as well. There is evidence that commodities lead bonds at secular turning points (Chart 5-4).

The two previous secular bull markets in bond yields were preceded by a secular low in commodity prices. Are commodities going to lead yields once again? Of course when we are limited to just two data points, we have to be careful about making projections. But the seven-year lead between the 2001 secular low in commodities and the late 2008 low for yields is certainly consistent with the two prior instances.

CHART 5-4 **U.S. Government Bond Yields Compared to Commodity Prices**
Commodity prices lead bond yields at secular turning points. Will the 2001 secular low in commodities lead to substantially higher government bond yields once again?

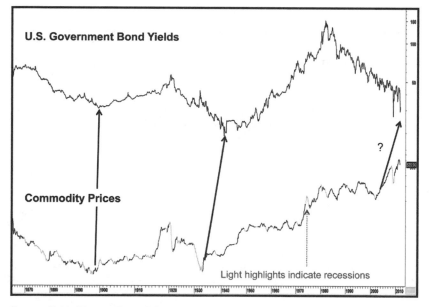

Source: Pring Turner Capital Group

The Ultimate Inflation/Deflation Relationship

The ultimate inflation/deflation relationship in financial markets is between commodities and bonds as shown in Chart 5-5. When the ratio is rising, this indicates that commodities are outperforming bonds (inflationary); when it is falling, bonds are outperforming commodities (deflationary).

Typically an advancing ratio means that commodities are rising and that bonds are falling; however, this is not always the case. Commodities and bonds could both be rising with commodities advancing at a faster clip than bonds, or they could both be falling with commodities declining at a slower pace. Trendline violations in the ratio can provide reliable and usually timely secular

CHART 5-5 The Ultimate Inflation/Deflation Ratio
When the ratio is rising, commodities are outperforming bonds (inflationary), and when the ratio is falling, bonds are outperforming commodities (deflationary). The momentum oscillator of the ratio signals that commodities are in the early phase of outperformance over bonds.

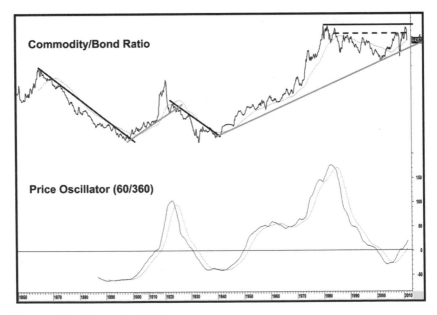

Source: Pring Turner Capital Group

trend reversal signals. This relationship understandably alternates between secular trends of inflation and deflation. However, since 1980 it has been in a wide trading range, almost breaking out to the upside in 2011, but just failing to surpass the 1980 high. If a (dashed) trendline is constructed in a slightly different way, the case for a breakout could have been argued at the time, but as you can see, this soon turned out to be a false signal. If it finally does move above its post–1980 trading range, it should be treated as a major long-term inflationary signal since it would denote the outperformance of commodities over bonds for years to come. Note that the long-term momentum oscillator (constructed by dividing a 60-month by a 360-month moving average of the ratio) in the lower panel is in the early phase of an advance as measured by its level compared to the elevated readings seen at previous inflationary sell signals. The relatively subdued reading at the start of 2012 also supports the view of an eventual upside resolution of the 1980–201? trading range in the commodity/bond ratio.

Finally, Chart 5-6 shows that secular trendline violations in the commodity/bond ratio have usually led to or coincided with trendline violations in the 20-year government bond yield series. Currently the trend for yields is down, and the 30-year trading range for the ratio is intact. However, we do have two very actionable points that when penetrated will strongly signal that an inflationary trend is underway.

Final Observations

Obviously our secular trend reversal signals have not yet been given, so we assume that the downtrend that began in 1981 is still intact. However, a piece of anecdotal evidence arguing in favor of a major peak in bond prices comes from the fact, not surprisingly, that markets usually reach their peak of popularity at their highest point.

CHART 5-6 The Ultimate Inflation/Deflation Ratio Versus Bond Yields
A strong inflationary trend will get underway should each of these series break out to the side. Bond owners should be on high alert and prepared to change tactics.

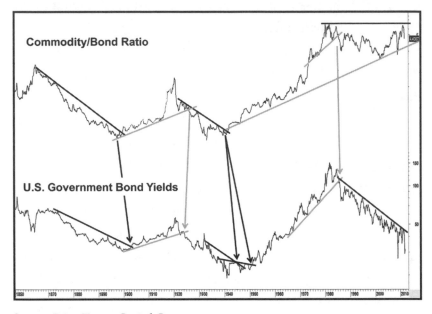

Source: Pring Turner Capital Group

At the culmination of the 1982–2000 secular bull market in stocks the Fidelity Magellan Fund (a stock fund) was the largest mutual fund in the world. In 2012 the largest mutual fund in the world is the PIMCO Total Return Fund—a bond fund! Perhaps when we get to the end of the secular bull market for commodities, the largest fund in the world will be commodity-related. Will precious metals, energy, or agricultural-related assets be the favored investment area as we approach a commodity secular top? Only time will tell, but our guess is that money will eventually flow from today's favorite (bonds) to commodities as the secular trends play out. After all, that is what human nature is all about. As individuals, we love to copy what the crowd is doing because that makes us feel comfortable. Prices consistently moving up for an extended period adds to our confidence, so at the final turning point we find forecasts and projections that would have seemed laughable at the beginning of the trend to be quite credible. With everyone around us expecting the same thing, it is very, no, *extremely* difficult to go against what has by now become conventional wisdom. This is what a secular turning point in commodities will be like.

But what of the secular bear market in yields (bull market in bond prices)? As stated earlier, the bull market in bonds is likely on its last legs. Certainly many of the long-term indicators are in position to signal the next reversal. U.S. financial history suggests that secular commodity price lows precede secular bottoms in interest rates. This is certainly consistent with the environment as the second decade of the twenty-first century is getting underway, considering that commodities bottomed in 2001. Once 30-year government bond yields give us a signal by breaking above 4.40 percent, your investment portfolio had better be prepared for substantially higher interest rates (lower bond prices), higher commodity prices, and an extension of the secular bear market in equities. While a new secular trend of rising rates will likely result in a substantial rise because it is a *secular* reversal, the trend will likely take place over the course of many decades.

This is the very subtle nature of secular trends; they creep up on you. However, in the early years following the reversal in trend, the rise in yields and commensurate decline in bond prices will present the kind of headwind investors have not experienced for many decades. Finally, when we look back at previous secular lows, we find that interest rates do not usually reverse on a dime but undergo an extended trading range spanning many years. If we assume that a trading range started in 2007 just prior to the financial crisis, it is quite credible that this trendless action could extend until the mid-part of the decade before rates and commodities take off on their respective secular bulls. We obviously cannot know this for sure. As long as the

30-year government yield remains below its 2007 levels, we will not have the evidence we need. In the meantime being forewarned and forearmed with this knowledge will make you better prepared for the investment battle that lies ahead. Now more than ever you cannot afford to sit back and relax, but you should prepare an investment plan for the second lost decade ahead bearing in mind the various possibilities.

KEY POINTS

1. As of the start of 2012, bonds have been in a 31-year secular bull market—investors must be on the alert for an important reversal.
2. Even a small rise in interest rates from these very low levels can lead to substantial bond portfolio losses.
3. An important intermarket relationship between commodities and bonds is in a massive trading range, but positive long-term momentum suggests that commodities will eventually win this battle.
4. Should the secular trend change be confirmed, you should adopt a more defensive approach in your bond portfolio tactics.

IMPORTANT QUESTIONS FROM THE SMITHS

What are the tactics we should use to protect our portfolio from a secular bear market in bonds when it happens?

Bonds come in many different forms—corporates, municipals, foreign, floaters, agencies, inflation-protected, and governments. For now let's focus on the U.S. Treasury market—the one asset class in the world considered the risk free safe haven. Can we still make that assessment? As previously discussed, the secular bull market for bonds has been going on for 31 years and is certainly getting long in the tooth. As of the beginning of 2012, 10-year yields are below 2 percent with 30-year yields at generational lows below 3 percent. Interestingly enough, these rather historic low yield levels were first reached in the summer of 2011 shortly after the Standard & Poor's rating agency decided to reduce the quality rating on Treasuries for the first time ever. The historic downgrade, issued in part because of concerns about the massive structural U.S. budget imbalances, moved the safety rating from AAA to AA. With some thanks to investor concerns over European sovereign debt problems and Dr. Ben Bernanke's Federal Reserve policies, bond yields ignored the news and declined, while prices climbed higher. How much longer will the secular bull market for bonds last? Is the U.S. Treasury market in a bubble? Nobody knows, but what we do know is that it is getting late in the secular trend and it makes sense to be on the alert for a potential trend change. In the meantime, what tactics can help protect bond portfolios?

A trend change away from the favorable environment for bond prices will require investors to carefully reevaluate their bond strategy since they will be faced with potentially devastating capital losses. This will involve both tactical and strategic portfolio adjustments. Basic changes for a hostile bond environment include: (1) reducing bond allocation percentage, (2) decreasing the average maturity of the bond portfolio, and (3) increasing exposure to inflation-sensitive investments to partially hedge the fixed income portion of the portfolio. One method for reducing the average maturity is to execute a short-term bond ladder that ensures full return of capital within a shortened time frame. This laddering strategy enables the investor to continuously roll over maturing bonds at higher and higher rates and protect principal values. TIPS are Treasury inflation-protected securities, such as *bonds, that do not pay much income, but principal values adjust to higher inflation rates. These bonds have not been around during wildly rising inflation periods, and in that sense they have not stood the test of time, but they do offer the investor an alternative to regular Treasuries and a fighting chance against inflationary periods. In addition, certain quality countries offer their own form of TIPS. For example, investments in Canadian and Australian inflation-protected securities offer inflation protection as well as a hedge against U.S. dollar weakness.*

What are some income-producing alternatives to bonds?

In the search for yield, investors must find alternatives to U.S. Treasury bonds, and sometimes that may come from unexpected places. For instance, emerging market government bonds are perceived as being riskier than Treasury bonds, but is this true? Which country would you rather invest in? One with historically low yields, high and growing debt loads, slow growth, and an aging population? Or one with attractive yields, low debt loads, faster-growing economies, and a young workforce? We would argue that there is a place in portfolios for emerging market debt (some ETFs do this in either U.S. dollars or local currency forms). Another alternative is the corporate bond area, where there is a distinct yield advantage over Treasuries. The balance sheets of many corporations have improved in recent years to the extent that they are in better financial health than the public sector. Which would you prefer to own in your portfolio, Greek government bonds or IBM corporate bonds?

High yield corporates can be sensitive to stock market swings, but a case can be made for including a basket of lower-quality corporate bonds to portfolios for the yield boost. For those in higher tax brackets, municipal bonds show good value with yields at or above U.S. Treasuries and with the added advantage of being tax-free. In this respect we would caution investors to be very selective because not all municipals are created equal. A general rule of thumb is to focus on stronger issues like general obligation bonds. These are backed by full taxing powers and secured by tax revenues. Additionally "essential purpose revenue" bonds, backed by a revenue stream from an essential service (like water, sewer, and toll districts), are also deemed safe, especially compared to just about every other municipal bond.

At the other end of the spectrum there are plenty of IOUs and promises to pay types of issues where local council members or politicians are required to appropriate funds each year to make interest and principal payments. That's not a terribly comforting feeling for investors considering the stress on municipal budgets recently. And of course, bond insurance is of virtually no value since many of the insurers have limited reserves to cover losses should a large default come along. If the underlying security is high quality, backed by tax revenues or stable revenue streams, and has insurance, then that is all well and good. But we wouldn't recommend an issue just based on the insurance.

Finally, we recommend exposure to high-quality, dividend-paying stocks, especially from those companies with long histories of stable and rising dividends. Many global blue chip companies have higher yields (with growing dividend streams) than U.S. Treasuries. Patient investors with long-term time horizons will very likely do well relative to Treasuries from these low yield levels. These types of companies are considered "core holdings" for us and act as a stable foundation for conservative portfolios. Yes, from time to time they may experience sharp price declines temporarily, but in the longer run they should win out over Treasuries.

The last secular change for bonds from good to bad was in the 1940s. What caused it, and what would cause interest rates to start going up now?

Each secular change is unique and has its own reasons for establishing a long-term turning point. The next major trend change for bonds will also be different. In the case of the bond market in the 1940s, interest rates on Treasury yields had dropped precipitously during the deflationary period of the Great Depression and stayed at very low levels into the early 1940s. As World War II ended, the U.S. economy surged during the global rebuilding effort with U.S. manufacturers being one of the biggest beneficiaries. Additionally, as troops returned from the war to start new households, the homebuilding and consumer sectors of the economy ran at near full capacity. Eventually, the deflationary environment of the 1930s gave way to a post-WWII inflationary one as each business cycle saw higher and higher interest rates (and lower and lower bond prices). Massive government spending for the war and the printing of additional dollars to fund it eventually led to a rising interest-rate environment. Today's concern is that the U.S. government (along with the Europeans) is in a similar position, printing more dollars to monetize excessive government debt levels that will ultimately lead to higher inflation and interest rates. Only time will tell exactly when that will occur, but one must be on the alert for signs of an important secular trend change for inflation, and this has vital consequences for bond investors.

CHAPTER 6

INTRODUCTION TO THE BUSINESS CYCLE

Harnessing business cycle knowledge is the most powerful tool an investor can utilize to successfully balance risk and reward in portfolios. Unfortunately, real-world knowledge and understanding of business cycles is greatly undervalued by consumers, business owners, and, most important, investors. How can you capture the power that changes in business activity provide? This chapter presents the practical value of applying basic business cycle knowledge to take advantage of profitable opportunities to enhance and protect personal net worth.

Earlier, in Chapter 2, we defined in the simplest terms what a business cycle is. First, in this chapter we further define and illustrate the typical four- to five-year business cycle. Second, we offer methods to identify where we are in the various stages or progress of business activity. Third, we demonstrate the usefulness of following business-cycle progress and how it can be used to make strategic asset allocation decisions.

What Is a Business Cycle?

Let's start with the textbook definition of a business cycle as defined in *Measuring Business Cycles* by Arthur F. Burns and Wesley C. Mitchell

(1946) and published by the National Bureau of Economic Research (NBER), which is the arbiter of dating the start and end of business cycles:

> Business cycles are a type of fluctuation found in the aggregate economic activity of nations that organize their work mainly in business enterprises: a cycle consists of expansions occurring at about the same time in many economic activities, followed by similarly general recessions, contractions and revivals which merge into the expansion phase of the next cycle.

In other words, the business cycle is the normal, sequential, and repeated ups and downs of the economy. The simplest representation of it is a bell-shaped curve. The shape is simple and elegant and implies continuous change, with one cycle leading into the next (see Figure 6-1).

The uphill (top) half of the curve implies the growth or expansion phase of the economy and historically lasts longer than the downhill (bottom) half. This a profitable time for companies, and the employment picture is bright. The bottom half of the bell-shaped curve, or contraction phase, is commonly referred to as a *recession*. A recession sees business activity shrinking. Sales and profits decline for corporations. As companies lay off employees, the unemployment rate climbs and household income declines. Recessions tend to expose, purge, and correct excesses that took place during the prior expansion. Both sides of a business cycle are self-adjusting or self-correcting mechanisms. For example, consumers who postponed spending on goods and services as long as they could during a recession must eventually replace worn-out goods, restock empty cupboards, and purchase deferred services. Once consumer spending begins again, low corporate inventory levels need to be replenished and hiring begins anew—the birth

FIGURE 6-1 Typical Business Cycle

The simple bell-shaped curve illustrates continuous change in the economy with one cycle leading into the next. Investors can benefit by observing the normal, sequential, and repetitive nature of the economy.

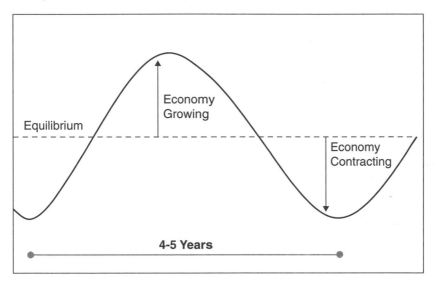

Source: Pring Turner Capital Group

of the next business expansion. The business cycle is continuous and has repeated over and over since the United States became an industrialized nation in the mid-1800s.

Our observation is that it is natural for people (the media especially) to take any recent economic trend and extrapolate that condition indefinitely into the future. If the nation is in the throes of a recession, people extrapolate the country's weak condition as though the recession will only worsen and never end. For instance, after months of bad news and a sinking stock market, you can imagine what negative emotions folks like the Smiths are experiencing. Concern, doubt, and paralyzing fear are deeply felt emotions that reflect a sense that the economy will never, ever recover. But just as day follows night, and negative emotions peak, the recession comes to an end and *merges into the expansion phase of the next cycle.* Times change as do economic leadership and news headlines, but human emotion around the business cycle will never change. We have witnessed stock investors being panicked and paralyzed near the bottom of a recession time and time again—just as the economy is about to turn up. By predicting economic turning points, investors can benefit greatly because the stock market is nothing more than fear and greed superimposed on the business cycle.

The exact opposite is also true at the top of business cycles when the belief and mantra is, "Business is great. Things couldn't get any better." Headlines will be rosy, unemployment low, and the talking heads on television will be looking at how high stock prices will go. Investors should take heed from such rosy conditions and forecasts. But instead of running from those words, they readily accept the rosy scenario and extrapolate that good times will go on forever. Never mind that at that point, the dependable and repeated history of business cycles demonstrates that investors should be looking for evidence of the cycle rolling over into the next slowdown and the arrival of the next bear market. The simplicity and beauty of keeping the bell-shaped curve of the business cycle in mind results in investors anticipating the next turning point in the cycle rather than their simply extrapolating recent conditions into the future.

A detailed historical analysis from the NBER (Table 6-1) indicates 33 completed business cycles dating back to the 1850s, when the United States first entered the industrial age. Understanding the sequences of the cycle allows investors to more carefully allocate assets around these four- to five-year cyclical swings in economic activity. The economy consists of indicators that lead us into the recovery (housing starts), those that coincide (nonfarm payrolls), and still others that follow behind (unemployment). Oftentimes housing will be moving up while some of the lagging indicators are declining, so what is this "economy" we are referring to? The answer

TABLE 6-1 NBER Business Cycle Reference Dates

The repetitive business cycle (ebb and flow of economic activity) sequence is a fact of life. Harnessing business cycle knowledge is the most powerful tool an investor can apply to portfolio management.

Cycle #	Peak*	Trough*	Cycle Duration (Peak to Peak)
1	June 1857(II)	December 1858 (IV)	
2	October 1860(III)	June 1861 (III)	3 Yrs 4 Months
3	April 1865(I)	December 1867 (I)	4 Yrs 6 Months
4	June 1869(II)	December 1870 (IV)	4 Yrs 2 Months
5	October 1873(III)	March 1879 (I)	4 Yrs 4 Months
6	March 1882(I)	May 1885 (II)	8 Yrs 5 Months
7	March 1887(II)	April 1888 (I)	5 Yrs
8	July 1890(III)	May 1891 (II)	3 Yrs 4 Months
9	January 1893(I)	June 1894 (II)	2 Yrs 6 Months
10	December 1895(IV)	June 1897 (II)	2 Yrs 11 Months
11	June 1899(III)	December 1900 (IV)	3 Yrs 6 Months
12	September 1902(IV)	August 1904 (III)	3 Yrs 3 Months
13	May 1907(II)	June 1908 (II)	4 Yrs 8 Months
14	January 1910(I)	January 1912 (IV)	2 Yrs 8 Months
15	January 1913(I)	December 1914 (IV)	3 Yrs
16	August 1918(III)	March 1919 (I)	5 Yrs 7 Months
17	January 1920(I)	July 1921 (III)	1 Yr 5 Months
18	May 1923(II)	July 1924 (III)	3 Yrs 4 Months
19	October 1926(III)	November 1927 (IV)	3 Yrs 5 Months
20	August 1929(III)	March 1933 (I)	2 Yrs 10 Months
21	May 1937(II)	June 1938 (II)	7 Yrs 9 Months
22	February 1945(I)	October 1945 (IV)	7 Yrs 9 Months
23	November 1948(IV)	October 1949 (IV)	3 Yrs 9 Months
24	July 1953(II)	May 1954 (II)	4 Yrs 8 Months
25	August 1957(III)	April 1958 (II)	4 Yrs 1 Month
26	April 1960(II)	February 1961 (I)	2 Yrs 8 Months
27	December 1969(IV)	November 1970 (IV)	9 Yrs 8 Months
28	November 1973(IV)	March 1975 (I)	3 Yrs 11 Months
29	January 1980(I)	July 1980 (III)	6 Yrs 2 Months
30	July 1981(III)	November 1982 (IV)	1 Yr 6 Months
31	July 1990(III)	March 1991(I)	9 Yrs
32	March 2001(I)	November 2001 (IV)	10 Yrs 8 Months
33	December 2007 (IV)	June 2009 (II)	6 Yrs 9 Months
Average	1857–2009 (33 cycles)		4 Yrs 8 Months

*Quarterly dates are in parentheses.

Source: National Bureau of Economic Research

is the indicators that move in the middle—the coincident indicators. In this respect GDP (gross domestic product) numbers would be a good start, so when we use the term "the economy," that's what we are referring to.

How Can an Investor Make Sense of the Economy?

Unfortunately in the real world the Smiths cannot count on the media or news sources to identify the prevailing stage of the business cycle. This is because the media tend to jumble the information flow around the economy and offer little help in understanding a useful sequence for putting the data in a sensible order. In fact, around crucial economic turning points the view of the media is likely to be wrong and unintentionally misleading. It is a good idea to look at the tangled knot of economic information for yourself, extract the important items, and try to place them properly in order of importance. Only then can that information be translated into a useful portfolio management strategy. Fortunately, thanks to a rich history of information going back over 150 years, it is possible to identify the sequence to the flow of financial and economic data. This can help you determine where we are on the bell-shaped curve.

If we just take a number of economic and financial indicators and overlay them on each other as shown in Chart 6-1, it looks like a real mess. But let us untangle the economic knot (as shown in Chart 6-2) and uncover the simple sequence of events that illustrates the progress a business cycle takes. Arrows are added to identify the sequential nature of the cycle, which now becomes more obvious. Solid arrows join the troughs, while dashed arrows connect the peaks. It should be noted that these are not the actual numbers but the indicators expressed as a deviation from trend or smoothed momentum. This is what gives a cyclic feel to the chart and puts us in a far better position to observe the logical, rational, and sequential turning points.

CHART 6-1 Random Noise of Economic News

Business activity is never smooth, and investors are continually bombarded with economic noise. How can an investor make sense of this tangled "economic Gordian knot"?

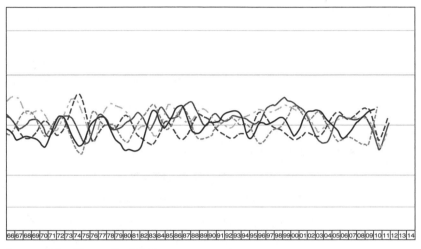

66|67|68|69|70|71|72|73|74|75|76|77|78|79|80|81|82|83|84|85|86|87|88|89|90|91|92|93|94|95|96|97|98|99|00|01|02|03|04|05|06|07|08|09|10|11|12|13|14

Source: Pring Turner Capital Group

CHART 6-2 Real-World Business Cycle Sequence

Separating the momentum of economic indicators and placing them in sequence brings clarity to the random noise. Business cycle turning points are readily identified, and the next step can be forecast, giving investors an important edge.

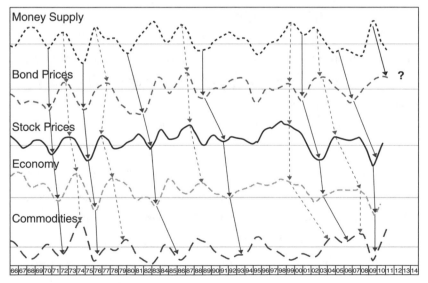

66|67|68|69|70|71|72|73|74|75|76|77|78|79|80|81|82|83|84|85|86|87|88|89|90|91|92|93|94|95|96|97|98|99|00|01|02|03|04|05|06|07|08|09|10|11|12|13|14

Source: Pring Turner Capital Group

Note that the slope of the arrows differs because the leads and lags change from cycle to cycle. The sequence is not perfect, but it repeats a majority of the time, and this is a tremendous advantage.

The business cycle sequence starts with money supply—the grease that keeps the economy moving. Assume that the economy is in recession and that the Federal Reserve is acting to stimulate growth. It will use various tactics to stimulate the economy, all of which have the effect of injecting liquidity into the banking system. In turn this lowers the level of interest rates and raises bond prices After a lag, the next step sees common stock prices bottom. Investors start to sniff out the next recovery, and stock prices advance as investors make their purchases ahead of the actual turn in the economy. Eventually the expansion in money supply, lower interest rates, and newly developed optimism around a rising stock market lead to the next economic recovery.

After a period of stronger economic growth, commodity prices strengthen resulting from increased demand and a slightly tighter supply situation in most cases. Now all three asset classes are appreciating—first bonds, then stocks, and eventually commodities. If commodity prices and other symptoms of price inflation intensify to an unacceptably high level, the Federal Reserve will at some point decide to take the punch bowl away from the party and head off an inflationary spiral. This step, therefore, sees the supply of credit tighten a bit as the Fed moves to a less accommodating stance. Simultaneously the demand for credit in the form of bank loans starts to pick up. This tightening balance between supply and demand ultimately raises interest rates and lowers bond prices. Equities dislike rising rates because they eventually result in an economic slowdown or actual contraction. However, at this point rates are rising slowly but corporate profits are growing even more, so it's a positive stage for stocks. As the rise in rates eventually accelerates, the economy will suffer and investors will start to foresee the next recession—just as they had anticipated the recovery. Stock investors will now factor in a potential recession or significant slowdown in the economic growth rate. Finally, as the economy slows, demand for raw materials declines and commodity prices peak and start to head lower. When it becomes evident that the economy is either slowing significantly or actually contracting, the Fed becomes more concerned about unemployment than inflation. Coming full circle, the next step will be to restimulate the economy once again, and a new business cycle begins.

How Can Business Cycle Awareness Be Useful?
Let us bring the Smiths back into the picture now that they have a better understanding and appreciation of the repetitive and sequential nature of business action. How can the Smiths use what they have learned to enhance their net worth and financial well-being?

The Smiths wear many different economic hats just like the rest of us do. They are consumers, spenders, savers, debtors, tax payers, businesspeople, and, most important, investors. For example, from a consumer point of view the best time to purchase a new vehicle is during a recession. This may sound counterintuitive, but during recessions auto manufacturers and dealers typically offer significant discounts or rebates, even zero percent financing on occasion. House prices are most attractive to a seller near the top of business cycles when optimism rules and prosperity is projected to go on forever. Home buyers will also find recessions to be favorable as pessimism and fear dominate sellers. Additionally this is the best time for homeowners to refinance and lower their mortgage rate, because interest rates have dropped. In contrast, the best time to lock in a favorable interest rate on a bank CD is just after the height of the cycle, when commodity prices have peaked but interest rates are still running wild on the upside.

Wouldn't it make sense for business owners to track the business cycle? It could alert them to be cautious and build up cash reserves at its height. Then, when things take a turn for the worse, they can use that cash to acquire a deeply discounted competitor or expand their plant and equipment when others are experiencing hard times and are motivated to strike a good deal in order to keep as many of their workers employed as possible. Of course that's easier said than done because business cycle peaks by definition are filled with extreme optimism. Therefore, it's very difficult to go against the trend. Similarly, when things are bleak, it takes a great deal of courage to take positive actions against the pessimistic conventional wisdom and the invariably depressing headlines. Indeed, we can go so far as to say if you do not feel uncomfortable going against the conventional wisdom, it is probably because things are not bleak enough yet. By definition, if it is a true bottom, everyone will feel uncomfortable. However, this was the approach taken by steel magnate Andrew Carnegie in the nineteenth century and by such great investors as Warren Buffett because going against the crowd became second nature to them.

In a secular bear market, business cycle analysis becomes more important than ever. If the lessons of secular history play out, then the second decade of the twenty-first century will experience increased business cycle volatility similar to that in the 1970s. Our research shows that economic recoveries will be briefer and contractions more extended, which means that retirees like the Smiths will need to be more nimble and opportunistic during cyclical bull markets and far more defensive during the longer and deeper periods of economic contraction.

Hopefully you are now in a better position to understand how business cycle dynamics can help you form important asset allocation decisions that will improve performance and reduce risk. A better appreciation of the business cycle before the last decade would have helped a lot of people sidestep *some* of the carnage from the two recessions and twin 50 percent-plus bear markets. The word *some* is deliberately italicized because we do not want to give you the impression that there is a perfect world out there, where everything operates according to theory. This is just not the case. Remember, our objective is not to identify exact turning points in the expectancy that profits and opportunities can be maximized because that's an investment mission impossible. What investors can do though is to try to smooth the rough edges. Just a couple of extra percentage points here and there each year will result in substantially greater long-term returns. Investing around the business cycle is your ticket to those annual incremental improvements in returns.

The next few chapters offer an expanded level of business cycle knowledge which will further your understanding of asset behavior around the typical cycle. We like to call it rational, logical, and sequential. With a deeper understanding of the sequences, we are confident that you will be able to make better investment decisions to build your portfolio values while taking less risk.

KEY POINTS

1. Markets have tracked business cycle sequences for over 150 years, basically since the industrialization of the economy.
2. Financial markets are linked rationally, logically, and sequentially to the business cycle.
3. Paying attention to the normal cyclical swings in the economy is an enormous help to investors, consumers, and business owners.

IMPORTANT QUESTIONS FROM THE SMITHS

We are concerned the business cycle doesn't work anymore. There are so many influences on the economy and the markets that make today different. Isn't it really different this time?

One of the benefits of studying business cycle history is the observation that if you go back far enough in time, you find that similar difficult periods have indeed happened. History is full of other episodes of financial crises, banking system meltdowns, government debt defaults, debt-deleveraging periods, and prolonged slow growth economies. Each secular bear period is unique, and its causes and circumstances differ. However, they are self-correcting mechanisms that clear the excesses of the prior bull period and set the stage for the next secular bull market to begin. The U.S. economy has demonstrated a tremendous ability to reboot, clean up past mistakes quickly, and reinvent itself. For investors, it is important to be able to observe the secular trend changes and then adopt new tactics to handle them. The last secular bear period in this country began in the 1960s, so it is easy to understand why many people may not be comfortable dealing with a deeply cyclical economy and market. Most of today's active investors are too young or were paying little attention to market behavior 40-plus years ago, which is a principal reason why they are unprepared for the current difficult environment. Just remember though that however bad things were in the past, the system eventually self-corrected and set the path for the next recovery.

CHAPTER 7

HOW THE BUSINESS CYCLE CAN BE USED AS A ROAD MAP FOR INVESTING IN BONDS, STOCKS, AND COMMODITIES

The last chapter introduced us to the idea that the business cycle is continually repeating in a logical and sequential manner as some economic indicators, such as housing starts, lead the recovery and others, such as capital spending and the unemployment numbers, follow way behind. If we can pinpoint when a specific indicator has just turned and we know the direction of the trend of several others, we can use this whole framework as a road map to help us understand where we are in the business cycle and, more important, what is likely to happen next. The good news for investors is that the turning points of the three financial markets also form part of this sequential process. First bonds bottom, then stocks, and finally commodities. Then the whole process is repeated for the three peaks.

Armed with this knowledge of the chronological bond, stock, commodity sequence, we are able to create an actual financial map. We know there are three markets and that each one has two turning points—a top and a bottom—resulting in six turning points in each cycle. For the Smiths, it may be easiest to understand how financial assets relate to cycles by thinking in terms of the seasons of the calendar year.

The Seasonal Nature of the Business Cycle

Back in the early 1990s Martin Pring wrote a book titled *The All-Season Investor* (Wiley, 1992) in which he in part explained the repeating and sequential relationship between the different asset class performances in the business cycle. He referenced how the calendar year has four seasons, each of which has its own characteristics. The metaphor serves as an excellent way to better understand investing around a business cycle.

The Smiths enjoy their family vegetable garden and over the years take pride in planning, caring for, and reaping the rewards of their careful attention. They also understand that they need the right tools and knowledge to successfully manage the plot. In the spring, when the climate improves from the cold winter months, they till the soil and plant the seeds for the growing season. In the summer months the tending chores shift to weeding, watering, and fertilizing to nurture the crop along. In the fall, the reward for all the hard work is an abundant supply of fresh vegetables to enjoy and share with family and friends. Finally, the winter months are a time to relax, perhaps sharpen the garden tools, and prepare for the next planting season a few months away.

Like the seasons of the year, the environment for bonds, stocks, and commodities also changes in a repeatable and sequential fashion. The Smiths, like a majority of investors out there, are unaware of and unprepared for the ever-changing financial market seasons. Importantly, they are not even sure of the right tools to use to tend to their finances. Their gardening experience tells them that it is useless to plant in the winter when the snow is on the ground because it is not the right season to do this. Planting seeds when it is too cold for them to germinate makes no agricultural sense at all. The same is true for the financial seasons in the business cycle. By better understanding these financial seasons and using the correct tools, the Smiths can make well-informed decisions and dramatically improve their chances for investment success.

Indeed, investors can use knowledge of the chronological bond, stock, and commodity sequence to create an actual financial map. We like to refer to the components as the three main food groups: bonds, stocks, and commodities or inflation-sensitive investments. Each one has two turning points in a given business cycle—a top and a bottom. This means that a typical cycle has six turning points—buy and sell for each of the three asset classes. We call these the *six stages*. The calendar year has four seasons, each of which has its own characteristics. The same can be said for the typical four- to five-year business cycle, which has six stages. We will explain the important historical features of each stage and how understanding the sequence can be invaluable to the successful rotation of assets.

In this chapter we describe the various stages, together with some of their broader implications for investment. Later on the discussion will turn to the more practical subject of how these stages may be identified as well as a description of the indicators to help you accomplish this task.

The Six Stages

The six stages of the business cycle are illustrated in Figure 7-1. The cycle begins with bonds in a bottoming mode and continues all the way through until the eventual peak in commodity prices.

The figure shows an idealized situation that does not necessarily develop exactly according to plan in the real world. To start with, it implies that each stage is equal in duration, but in reality this is not the case. Occasionally two markets may reverse simultaneously. This is what happened in October 1966 when both bonds and stocks bottomed together. In such a situation the cycle moves from stage 6, when all three markets are declining, directly to stage 2 where bonds

FIGURE 7-1 Pring Turner's Six Business Cycle Stages
Follow the business cycle sequence to dynamically adjust asset allocations and
emphasize or deemphasize each asset class for optimal risk-adjusted returns.

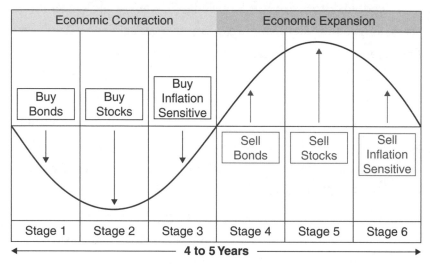

Source: Pring Turner Capital Group

and stocks are bullish and commodities bearish. Stage 1, in which
bonds are bullish and the other two markets are bearish, is therefore bypassed. On the other hand, there was an almost two-year lag
between the 1984 low in stocks and the 1986 bottom in commodities.

It is not unprecedented for the markets themselves to reverse
direction out of sequence. Commodities bottomed ahead of stocks
in 1937. This turned out to be an unusually bullish situation since
it represented the early years of a multidecade rise in commodity
prices. While not normal, it nonetheless serves as a reminder that the
sequential approach described here is by no means automatic. If it
worked like clockwork in every cycle, everyone would be using this
approach and it would be instantly discounted. Our research indicates that the six stages move sequentially approximately 85 percent
of the time. This knowledge is an enormous edge for investors. These
concepts should therefore be used as an overall basis for analysis
and investment policy, but not to the total exclusion of independent

thinking. The rest of this chapter is devoted to a description of the kind of investment environment that can be expected at each stage. Afterward we will be in a position to look at some ways in which the stages can be identified.

A General Overview

Figure 7-2 shows the bell-shaped curves for the three asset classes (bonds, stocks, and commodities). Since each one dances to the beat of a different drummer in the business cycle, there are times when they are moving in different trajectories and times when they are all operating in the same direction. The two highlighted boxes indicate periods when all three markets are either rising or falling simultaneously—stages 3 and 6, respectively.

FIGURE 7-2 Theoretical Bell Curves for Bonds, Stocks, and Commodities
The three asset classes move in different trajectories during the typical business cycle. The shaded boxes indicate periods when all three markets are either rising or falling simultaneously. The rest of the time they tend to move in different trajectories.

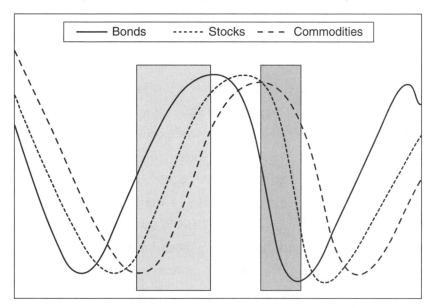

Source: Pring Turner Capital Group

FIGURE 7-3 Pring Turner's Six Business Cycle Stages
The six-stage model can help investors dynamically adjust asset allocations around the typical business cycle sequence. Essentially an investor needs two game plans: one for defense to protect assets in difficult periods and one for offense to grow wealth during favorable conditions.

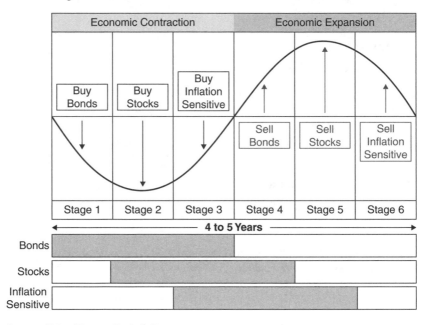

Source: Pring Turner Capital Group

Figure 7-3 demonstrates when the various assets should be emphasized. This is shown in the shaded boxes at the bottom of the diagram.

To review, the bell-shaped curve represents the ebbs and flows of business activity in the four- to five-year cycle. The left side starts with the economy in recession and is the starting point for our model. At this time bondholders have everything on their side. First, credit demand is falling like a stone because of the lackluster economy; businesses are battening down the hatches and paying down, not expanding debt. Second, the Fed is now committed to fighting the unemployment battle and is pumping money into the banking system as fast as it can. This falling demand and expanding supply of credit reduces its price (interest rates). Since bond prices move inversely with interest rates, this means that good-quality bonds will appreciate in value. From a risk versus reward standpoint stage 1 is generally good for bonds but not as kind to stocks and commodities.

Next, in the depths of recession and after interest rates have declined and bond prices appreciated, the stock market begins to turn up. This point befuddles most investors because the stock market begins a dynamic cyclical advance when the economic news cannot be any worse. A stock market bottom by definition is the point of maximum pessimism. Knowledgeable investors take advantage of the stock market's character to be one of the most dependable leading economic indicators. It still takes courage (and cash) to buy stock in the midst of miserable economic headlines. This is typical behavior for stage 2 where stocks start to show strong performance. At this point two asset classes are in cyclical bull markets, bonds and stocks, while commodities are still underperforming. As the economy picks up steam, the demand for raw materials increases, and finally commodity prices join the party. This is distinctive of a stage 3 environment, where all three asset classes are doing well, and everyone, including the Smiths, are investment geniuses.

Eventually, we have too much of a good thing as the economy and commodity prices heat up and inflationary forces take hold. This development gets the attention of the Federal Reserve. Taking its cue from rising inflation, the Fed begins the process of tightening monetary conditions and starts to raise interest rates for this cycle. This action immediately affects bond prices negatively and signals the typical stage 4 where bonds do poorly, but stocks and commodities continue to rally. When rates move high enough, the stock market eventually takes notice and prices turn down in anticipation of an oncoming economic slowdown. Stage 5 is now positive only for commodities, as bonds and stocks begin their cyclical declines. Finally, sagging demand for resources resulting from the slowing economy pushes commodities into their cyclical downturn, and now in stage 6 all three asset classes are in bear markets. The cycle is complete, and the next step is to anticipate the move back to stage 1 for a repeat of the process.

Some of you more observant readers may be asking about any other possible combinations that may fall outside the theoretical six-stage model. In fact, there are two other potential scenarios to look for when the asset classes get out of sequence. This happens when bonds and commodities are bearish leaving stocks bullish, and when bonds and commodities are bullish and stocks are bearish. We refer to these as stages 7 and 8 and acknowledge that while these two do not happen very often (about 10 percent of the time), they certainly need to be taken into consideration.

When you think about it, the cycle can really be split into two parts—an inflationary part and a deflationary one. This is shown in Figure 7-4, where the vertical partition serves as a rough guide for

FIGURE 7-4 Deflationary and Inflationary Parts of the Business Cycle
During the deflationary stage, bonds and defensive high-dividend stocks are appropriate. The inflationary stage should emphasize commodity ETFs or resource-based and basic industry stocks.

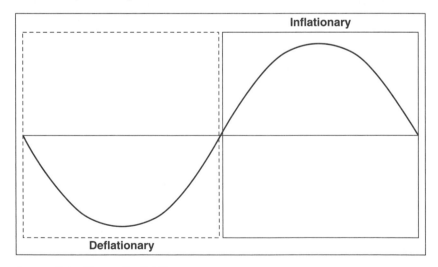

Source: Pring Turner Capital Group

asset allocation. During the deflationary stage, bonds and defensive and high-dividend stocks would be appropriate. However, in the inflationary stage exposure to commodity ETFs, resource-based and basic industry stocks, and so on make more sense.

Now that we have outlined this rather stark contrast between the basic dual phases of the cycle, it makes sense to discuss some rudimentary aspects of asset allocation around the stages. The material covered in this chapter is general in nature but don't worry. If you want to drill down more on this subject, we have included a more detailed account in Appendix D.

Applying Business Cycle Stage Shifts to Asset Allocation Changes

The key point in applying cycle stage shifts to changes in asset allocation is viewing asset allocation within the context of understanding the risk and reward characteristics of the different asset classes at each stage of the economic cycle. (See Table 7-1.)

For instance, during a recession in stage 1 the allocation includes a healthy mix of bonds and cash to stabilize portfolio values. The opposite is true in stage 3, when the economy is running at full throttle and maximum exposure to stocks is recommended. Doesn't it make sense to reduce exposure to stocks in anticipation of a recession and to reemphasize them just prior to when the economy is expected to accelerate into a growth mode? In this sense important asset

TABLE 7-1 Broad Business Cycle Asset Allocation Guidelines
This broad asset allocation guideline can serve as an important starting point for actively managing portfolios throughout the business cycle.

Stage	1	2	3	4	5	6
Bond Allocation	30%–50%	10%–30%	10%–30%	10%–25%	10%–30%	20%–40%
Stock Allocation	30%–50%	65%–85%	60%–80%	60%–80%	40%–60%	20%–40%
Cash Allocation	10%–30%	0%–15%	5%–20%	10%–20%	20%–40%	20%–40%

Source: Pring Turner Capital Group

allocation decisions are not static rules based solely on your age and risk temperament. Instead, asset levels should be actively changed based on the historical risk/reward relationship of each level around the normal cyclical swings in the economy and financial markets. We believe that our six-stage framework is an ideal way to construct an active allocation discipline, especially because it also serves as a critical risk-management tool.

However, it is important to remember that no strategy or discipline is perfect and that each has its own shortcomings. In the case of economic fluctuations, not all cycles will experience every stage, and stages occasionally diverge from the expected sequential order. Sometimes the cycle will skip a stage or even two. In fact a cycle may also retrograde to a previous phase. Another drawback is that a lot of specific stages will be identified only after they have been under way for some time. These are additional reasons why changes to portfolio allocations should be gradual. You should take into account other considerations, including market action itself. Finally, larger allocation switches can be justified only when the evidence of a change in the environment is overwhelming and markets have not already gone too far in factoring this into prices. Nonetheless, over several decades the investment management team at Pring Turner Capital Group has found the methodology to be an invaluable tool in successfully managing client portfolios while taking less overall market risk. For investors, the beauty of following the repetitious nature of the business cycle is an investment methodology that never goes out of style.

In the next chapter we will further study the historical performance data of stocks, bonds, and commodities and give you more tools to help you use the business cycle to your best advantage. We will explain a "quick test" to help you easily identify what stage of the cycle we are in. Going a step further, we will also share invaluable sector performance data around the stages that can help you detect the best and worst sectors for each stage of the business cycle. Sector emphasis around the cycle is an additional risk-management tool to drive even better performance while reducing risk.

KEY POINTS

1. We organize the business cycle into six stages to identify which asset class to favor or underweight in each stage.
2. During secular bear markets, the economy is often in recession, and business cycle analysis has added importance.
3. Optimal asset allocation for portfolios can be adjusted based on the business cycle stage in an effort to increase returns and reduce risks.

IMPORTANT QUESTIONS FROM THE SMITHS

We see that the average business cycle lasts between four and five years, yet between 1990 and 2001 there was no recession. Doesn't this question the validity of your thesis?

That is a great question. First, that period developed for the most part under the context of a secular bull market where recessions are shallow and far less common. Second, even during these long patches between recessions, the economic growth path slows down every four years or so. The difference is that growth slows, but it does not contract. We still get the bond and stock commodity sequence, but the difference is that equities avoid a full-fledged bear market. In 1994, for example, the average stock lost about 20 percent, and the market experienced a sideways trading range, not an extended decline as it probably would have experienced if a recession had emerged. Compare that to the 2008–2009 period when the economy declined sharply as did the stock market.

The business cycle research relating to the U.S. economy makes sense, but the rest of the world does not just revolve around the United States. Is your work still relevant as the global economy becomes more interconnected? How do you take advantage of growth outside the United States?

Your observation may be true to some extent, but the United States is still the largest economy in the world with significant corporate revenues being generated by overseas operations. Indeed, many of the largest companies in the United States have a greater contribution of sales from global markets than within our borders. Companies like Caterpillar, Coca-Cola, Intel, and Procter & Gamble are just a few of the global growth beneficiaries based in the United States. The important point is that just because we expect the U.S. economy to face headwinds in the second lost decade, global leadership companies are still likely to continue to see rising profits. Fortunately, you are able to invest in companies, not economies. In essence, global economies are tracking each other in a more correlated manner than ever before, and following the U.S. business cycle remains as important as ever. It is also quite evident that parts of the world are growing much faster than others. In very broad terms we can segregate those in secular bull markets from those in secular bears.

Many of the economies in the developed world are in secular bear markets and have been since 2000. This includes the United States, Western Europe, and Japan, whose economies share certain negative common characteristics—high debt, slow growth, aging populations, and persistent high unemployment. On the other hand, the economies experiencing secular bull behavior include the emerging economies in Asia, Latin America, and Eastern Europe. These developing countries have certain positive common characteristics—low debt, high growth, young populations, and strong job markets. In addition, a few resource-based developed countries like Canada, Australia, and South Africa offer opportunities to invest in areas that benefit from the continued infrastructure build-out taking place in the developing world.

From an investment standpoint there are some distinctions to make and considerations for portfolio managers. While the emerging markets show the highest growth potential, they have also exhibited the highest level of volatility. It is not unusual to find these markets with volatility readings (beta and standard deviations for instance) at 40 to 50 percent higher levels than the U.S. market. They exemplify the investment adage: higher risks for higher return potential. For example, when the U.S. markets drop by 20 percent, these high beta markets can decline by 30 percent or more. For conservative investors, this may be a bit more excitement than they bargained for. One solution is to take smaller bites for portfolio allocation purposes with the idea that a little bit can go a long way. Another suggestion is to view the investments as "tactical" buys for a shorter-term holding period. For instance, you may consider allocating 8 percent of a portfolio to Asian emerging markets. Then after you see them advance, you can trim the position back to 4 percent or even less. After an intermediate decline, the position can be fully established once again for the next intermediate up move. This viable tactic is called "trading around the core"—where a long-term "core" investment position is kept in a favorable secular bull market asset, but a tactical trading position is managed around the intermediate term (two to six months) and is especially important around the cyclical (four to five years) moves.

The key observation is that there are opportunities around the globe and within the United States for leading beneficiaries of the dynamic global growth occurring in emerging economies. Many U.S.-based companies offer a safer way to profit from this growth while sporting consistent earnings and dividend histories. Additionally, direct investments in *emerging markets have to be made with caution and the understanding that they can be substantially more volatile than the U.S. markets. At Pring Turner Capital Group we prefer using these markets as tactical plays where we move in and out based on our market outlook for each and the comparative relative strength characteristics versus the U.S. market.*

CHAPTER 8

HOW TO IDENTIFY THE BUSINESS CYCLE STAGES USING EASY-TO-FOLLOW INDICATORS

Previously we pointed out that the business cycle is really a road map for the financial markets and their interaction. In this chapter we present some ideas to help you identify where the cycle might be at any one point in time. This is certainly a legitimate question for our friends the Smiths, who may be wondering how they can possibly keep track of where they are in the business cycle. More to the point, they would want to know what stage they are in and where the risks and opportunities lie.

Some Background Factors

In our money management operation we have traditionally used models or barometers to determine the prevailing stage of the cycle. There are three barometers, one for each asset class: bonds, stocks, and commodities. Each is constructed from a variety of momentum, trend following, and inter-asset relationships. Their individual components have all been acceptably reliable over the years. However, because no individual indicator is perfect, we prefer to take a consensus approach. When the census is positive, the barometer is deemed to be bullish, and when it is negative, the barometer is bearish. When the bond barometer is positive and stocks and commodities are negative, this tells us that we are in stage 1. These barometers are kept up to date on a regular basis and are published on a monthly basis in *Martin Pring's InterMarket Review*. For nonsubscribers the calculation of these models would be somewhat laborious. Consequently, we have come up with some easy-to-follow guidelines to help you to come close to achieving the same objective.

Most business cycles experience six stages, as defined by the chronological sequence of market peaks and troughs, but some do not always follow the sequence. Consequently, it should never be assumed that this progression can be mechanically extrapolated in every cycle, because occasionally the expected chronology of actual peaks and troughs will not operate sequentially. Alternatively the stages may retrograde, for example, as the cycle moves from stage 3 back to stage 2 and then back to stage 3. Stages can also be skipped as the cycle jumps from, say, stage 6 to stage 2. The point we are making is that there is no such word as perfection in the investment business because we are dealing in markets, and markets are a reflection of people in action. Unfortunately, people can and do change their minds, therefore so do markets. We would love to tell you that the tools we describe in this chapter are guaranteed to work 100 percent of the time, but that's not the case. However, we can say that most of the time they will operate reliably, thereby putting the *probabilities* in your favor. The word *probabilities* has been deliberately emphasized because it summarizes our approach in a nutshell.

If each cycle repeated in chronological sequence and if there was no difference in leads, lags, and magnitude of market moves, our task would be pretty simple. Unfortunately, this is not the case. This is a major reason why it is important to rotate asset allocations in a slow and consistent manner. There are many times when the indicators offer clear-cut evidence that a specific stage has been reached.

However, more often than not, the market in question will already have moved before the evidence becomes conclusive. This is why it is mandatory to rotate the asset mix gradually. As more information becomes available, allocations can be incrementally increased or reduced. In this way you will be positioned and mentally prepared for the next step.

Anticipating the next market move is not unlike taking a long train journey. For example, you are closing in on your final destination and plan to get off at the next stop. You are probably very anxious not to miss your stop. Under such circumstances, chances are that you will get out of your seat as you sense the train approaching the station, grab hold of your luggage, and proceed to the door. You will not, of course, get out of the train until you know it has actually come to a complete stop, but you have nevertheless prepared yourself both mentally and physically to disembark immediately as the train arrives at your destination.

The same should be true of the asset rotation process, except to say that it is usually a good idea to begin shifting a few assets when you have grounds for suspecting that the cycle has started to move to the next stage. In some cases a partial rotation could be justified *ahead* of the markets, but it should never be done to the degree that your whole investment approach will be jeopardized in the event you are wrong. Put more kindly, investors do not bet their entire portfolio in the event that the markets do not respond as expected. The characteristics of each cycle are different, so it makes sense to set an allocation range rather than a specific number for a particular stage (e.g., 30 to 50 percent for bonds in stage 1, rather than, say, 40 percent).

Identifying Stages by Market Action

One way of classifying the stages is to look at the trend of the three asset classes. If all classes are bullish, this would be stage 3. If commodities are the only positive asset class, you are in stage 5 and so forth. Since we only know for sure that a market has peaked or troughed with the benefit of hindsight, we need some objective method to identify these trends. For the purposes of this exercise, we use the three main asset classes—bonds, stocks, and commodities—relative to their 12-month moving averages. A market that is above its moving average would be treated as bullish, and a market below its moving average is bearish. Thus, stage 1 is defined when bond prices are above their moving average and stocks and commodities are below theirs. Stage 6 is signaled when all three asset classes are below their respective moving averages.

The question may be asked, why a 12-month moving average? Why not some other average? The 12-month moving average was originally adopted because it includes every month in the calendar year and is therefore seasonally adjusted. This time span also tests consistently, but certainly not perfectly, for most security price trends. As an added checkpoint and because markets can swing above and below the average in whipsaw fashion, it is a good idea to check only month-end levels to gauge the reading.

Ideally we want to see an asset class move between a bullish and bearish reading twice in a four-year cycle (one buy and one sell for each asset class). Using this simple moving-average approach to identify the stages may give occasional whipsaw signals, but a vast majority of the time it works and is easy to follow. Table 8-1 provides a "quick test" example.

Table 8-2 is a "cheat sheet" to help you use moving averages to easily identify the business cycle stage.

The Results

One of the great advantages of using markets to identify the stages is that we can take the history back a long time, making it possible

TABLE 8-1 Quick Test: What Is the Current Business Cycle Stage?
Answer: At month-end, when bonds are above their 12-month moving average and stocks/commodities are below their respective 12-month averages, this quick test signals a stage 1 environment.

Asset Class	Above 12-Month Moving Average	Below 12-Month Moving Average
Bonds (TLT)*	✓	
Stocks (S&P 500)		✓
Commodities (CRB Raw Industrials)		✓

*iShares Barclays 20-year Treasury Bond
Source: Pring Turner Capital Group

TABLE 8-2 Cheat Sheet: What Is the Current Business Cycle Stage?
Use this handy cheat sheet to help identify the current business cycle stage.

Stage	1	2	3	4	5	6	7*	8*
Bonds (TLT)	+	+	+	−	−	−	−	+
Stocks (S&P 500)	−	+	+	+	−	−	+	−
Commodities (CRB Raw Industrials)	−	−	+	+	+	−	−	+

+Denotes that the asset class is above its 12-month moving average.
−Denotes that the asset class is below its 12-month moving average.
*Denotes an out-of-sequence stage in the business cycle.
Source: Pring Turner Capital Group

to test the concept over many secular trends, both inflationary and deflationary. The results for the 111-year period between 1900 and 2011 are shown in Table 8-3, where the stages are defined using asset class relationships with their respective 12-month moving averages.

Most of the results are as we might expect. However, we see that stocks put in a positive performance in stage 1, which should not be the case. The reason lies in the fact that normally when interest rates peak, stocks do not have very far to fall. At the same time, bear market bottoms are often followed by explosive advances, which means that equity prices have already advanced quite a way by the time they

TABLE 8-3 1900–2011 Total Return Asset Performance by Stage

Historical results where stages are defined using asset class relationship with their respective 12-month moving averages. Asset performance for each stage should be carefully weighed against volatility. Standard deviation (as shown in columns 2, 3, and 4) is a risk-management statistic—the lower the number, the lower the volatility (risk).

Stage	Bonds	Stocks	Commodities	% in Stage
1	+8.3% (9.8%)	+13.4% (24.5%)	−12.6% (11.8%)	10.2%
2	+9.2% (7.0%)	+22.4% (14.8%)	−0.1% (7.7%)	15.4%
3	+4.0% (6.3%)	+17.3% (12.3%)	+10.8% (8.5%)	18.4%
4	+2.6% (5.7%)	+10.1% (12.1%)	+9.4% (6.9%)	23.1%
5	+3.2% (5.8%)	−6.3% (15.5%)	+4.2% (8.7%)	12.1%
6	+9.7% (7.3%)	−3.4% (16.7%)	−9.4% (8.0%)	9.1%
7	+2.1% (5.5%)	+16.0% (14.7%)	+2.8% (5.8%)	7.6%
8	+5.0% (7.0%)	+7.1% (14.6%)	+10.4% (8.5%)	4.1%
Total	+5.2% (6.8%)	+10.4% (15.5%)	+2.8% (8.6%)	100%

Source: Pring Turner Capital Group

rally above their 12-month moving average. Think of the *real* stages, as determined by the actual turning points in the markets. This means that the stock market rally between the bear market low and the moving average crossover is really stage 2, but it is not recognized as such by our methodology until the crossover actually takes place.

Finally, the table also includes stages 7 and 8 because there are eight possible combinations, two of which fall outside our theoretical business cycle. This happens when bonds and commodities are bearish, leaving stocks bullish, and when bonds and commodities are bullish and stocks bearish. This does not happen very often (about 10 percent of the time), but it needs to be taken into consideration.

You will note that in addition to showing the returns for each class by stage, we have also included the standard deviation as a measure of volatility to help the investor balance returns with the risk taken. As described later in Chapter 10 on risk management, the important consideration for investors is not only what return to expect but how much risk is involved to generate it. Although stocks may show positive performance in stage 1, periods when they are not supposed to do well, you will note that the standard deviation is also much higher than in other stages. That is not an ideal climate for conservative stock investors. We prefer to take a more aggressive stance on stocks when the returns are good *and* the volatility is low as in most stage 3s and 4s. The historical information in these tables is useful in helping you understand the important risk versus reward relationship between the three main asset classes and is a key factor in dynamic asset allocation decisions. Since these are average returns over all the stages since 1900, it is important to understand that not every stage will behave the same way in the future. Each cycle is different, but the repeatable sequence is rational and logical, and it works. History confirms that a business cycle investment approach provides solid investment profits with less risk. Isn't this the Smiths' ultimate investment goal?

Sector Performance Around the Stage Changes

Taking the historical data one step further, we also studied the performance of individual stock sectors in each of the six stages. It is widely known that certain sectors outperform at different times within the business cycle. Sectors are often categorized as "early cycle," "midcycle," or "late cycle" winners, and many portfolio managers take this into account when making sector rotation decisions. By breaking down sector *outperformance* and, just as important, *underperformance* within each stage, investors can further fine-tune portfolio allocations and sector emphasis. This can add yet another layer of risk management for even better risk/return outcomes. Table 8-4 shows the historical sector leaders and laggards by stage since 1955 as defined by our own barometer signals.

TABLE 8-4 Pring Turner's Six-Stage Sector Emphasis

Sector rotation through the business cycle stages will further improve performance and reduce risk. Not every cycle is the same; however, certain sectors historically outperform or underperform in each stage.

Stage	1	2	3	4	5	6
Best Performers	Home Builders	Brokers	Communication Equipment	Oil Drillers	Health Care	Household Products
	Restaurants	Automobiles	Diversified Metals	Computer Hardware	Diversified Chemicals	Life Insurance
	Utilities	Semiconductors	Energy	Gold Shares	Consumer Staples	Food Products
Worst Performers	Diversified Metals	Copper/Gold	Leisure	Hotels	General Merchandising	Chemicals
	Industrials	Oil Drillers	Airlines	Brokers	Automobiles	Railroads
	Communication Equipment	Energy	Home Furnishing	Home Building	Semiconductors	Steel Companies

Source: Pring Turner Capital Group

It is not intended to be used as a strict guide but rather as a starting point for potential sector allocations. For example, we learn that utilities do well in (deflationary) stage 1, so a serious allocation would be considered when it was felt that the cycle had reached this phase. However, before utilities could be purchased, we would need to take a look at their performance relative to the S&P Composite to make sure that indeed this sector was acting positively at a time when it should be. For example, it may be that at this particular time utilities are being shunned by the investment community because of fears of overregulation. If this is the case, that would mean lower profitability, smaller dividends, and so forth. In this instance, utilities would be deemphasized in favor of other sectors that do well at this time of the cycle, such as home builders.

We utilize other tools such as relative strength analysis to further identify leadership areas for the current stage and determine whether or not the expected groups are doing well. Relative strength analysis compares the performance of a sector against the overall market and plots the result as a continuous line. Trends in relative action are then appraised in the same way as any time series with moving averages, trendlines, and oscillators to help spot the outperformers. In a sense, this form of analysis can act as an important double-check to past performance and can either confirm or contradict the expected winners and losers. In the best circumstances, the current cycle outperformers will match up with history to give more confidence to investment decision making. However, if the current doesn't match up with past behavior, then it only makes sense to ignore history for this sector at this stage. Most important, with the stage work history as a guide, it is possible to better anticipate what sectors are *expected* to be the next outperformers and underperformers as the stages move progressively along. Relative strength analysis helps confirm or reject past results. To a large degree the historical data are very useful in the early identification process and serve to allow an investor to act with more conviction at critical business cycle turning points.

Now the Smiths have some new powerful tools and the awareness of how financial asset performance relates to the business cycle. The end result is that they have more confidence to conservatively manage their retirement portfolio around the ever-repeating ebbs and flows of the economy. Investment allocations can be made based on historical stage analysis and with full recognition of risk and reward trade-offs for each asset class at each stage. Instead of sticking with a static buy-and-hold approach where they are victims of the ongoing secular bear market, the Smiths feel empowered while utilizing a more flexible tactic by taking advantage of a dynamic asset allocation strategy. It allows them the opportunity to achieve better performance while taking less risk and, most important, with greater peace of mind.

KEY POINTS

1. Pring Turner's barometer models for identifying business cycle stages is a laborious task, but a quick and generally reliable test is to simply observe if each asset class is above or below its own 12-month moving average.
2. Historic returns by stage for each asset class since 1900 with volatility measures give investors important data so that they can set personal asset allocation guidelines that balance risk versus return.
3. Sectors behave differently in each stage, and historic analysis can identify likely winners and losers for each stage of the business cycle to further enhance returns.
4. Proactive asset allocation and sector rotation adjustments are key elements to building and protecting wealth in the continued secular bear market for stocks.

IMPORTANT QUESTIONS FROM THE SMITHS

What is your opinion on real estate, and how does it fit in the stages discussed?

First, regarding homes, in secular terms the recent housing collapse ranks as one of the worst bear markets since the early part of the last century. Since World War II, housing prices in real terms moved modestly higher until the late 1990s when a decade-long housing bubble formed that took prices 85 percent higher in the 10-year period ending in 2006 (S&P/Case-Shiller data).* Since the bubble peak in 2006, U.S. housing prices have declined by 40 percent in inflation-adjusted terms and at the start of 2012 sat at a price level similar to the one in 1999. The enormous shrinkage in homeowner equity has had a devastating economic impact as consumers are less wealthy and have lost a lot of confidence in the real estate market. At one time real estate was considered a sure thing, but that attitude has changed completely with new buyers very reluctant to take on large mortgages in order to acquire their dream home. We suspect that a lot of the work clearing out the enormous inventories of foreclosed homes has worked its way through the system and that the immediate post–2012 period could see a resumption of price stability. Longer term, the slow inflation-adjusted growth of 2 to 3 percent per year that occurred post-WWII would be expected.

Second, for investors, REITs (real estate investment trusts) are a liquid form of investing in various sectors of the real estate market. REITs often specialize in specific segments, like housing, apartments, commercial, industrial, retail, and other categories. Generally, well-capitalized REITs run by experienced management teams develop,

---

*The S&P/Case-Shiller Home Price Indices are the most accepted measures for the U.S. residential housing market, tracking changes in the value of residential real estate both nationally as well as in 20 metropolitan regions.

buy, and sell properties for the benefit of the shareholder. Often they generate attractive income from rents and have a natural inflation protection—cash flow to investors increases as rents rise. While REITs were not widely available prior to the 1970s and the very long-term trends cannot be measured, they have quickly become an integral part of the asset allocation of institutions and individuals searching for income and diversification from equities and bonds. Our stage work studies have not shown consistent patterns of outperformance or underperformance by stage for this broad group of real estate trusts, but it generally does act similarly to defensive areas of the market.

CHAPTER 9

INTRODUCING THE DOW JONES PRING BUSINESS CYCLE INDEX—THE ALL-SEASON ANSWER FOR THE SMITHS

The period between 2000 and 2011 was indeed a rough 12 years for the Smiths and other stock investors, including those who invested passively in an index fund. The challenge was even greater for active investors; the 20-year studies by market research firm Dalbar* show consistent underperformance for them. The average investor, without an understanding of the business cycle, tends to act on emotions and buys when prices are high and sells when they are low. The performance is even worse than a buy-and-hold approach because it shows significant underperformance to even the low returns of passive investors. As the title of this book suggests, investors are forewarned to prepare for a *second* rough decade with more recessions and continued emotional and volatile market conditions.

---

*The 2009 update of the Dalbar Quantitative Analysis of Investor Behavior (QAIB) Study measures performance over the 20-year period extending from January 1, 1989, through December 31, 2008. Over the 20 years ending December 31, 2008, equity mutual fund investors had average annual returns of only +1.87 percent while the S&P 500 index averaged +8.35 percent over the same time period. Fixed income fund investors had average annual returns of +0.77 percent over the same 20-year period, while the benchmark Barclays Aggregate Bond Index averaged +7.43 percent.

The solution is to adopt a systematic methodology for decision making that brings positive returns with less risk and emotional stress. Investors must recognize that there is no holy grail or perfect solution but that there are answers to sleepless nights and profit-less portfolios. The answers come from the information provided in prior chapters, which give the average investor an important edge in consistent portfolio performance. This is achieved by taking an "all-season" investment approach to proactively allocate assets and shift portfolio holdings around the sequential business cycle stages. The "all-season" term comes from the book *The All-Season Investor* (Wiley, 1992) written by Martin Pring.

By now the Smiths are saying to themselves that this whole approach makes great sense and sounds perfectly rational. But how does the theory presented in the book perform in the real world? Does it actually work? *The evidence is revealed in the new Dow Jones Pring Business Cycle Index!*

The Dow Jones Indexes organization, intrigued with our research, contacted Martin Pring in 2010 to explore the possibility of using the unique six-stage strategy to produce a business cycle index. Dow Jones Indexes, after thoroughly backtesting the barometer data and research theory going back to 1955, determined that the methodology indeed improves performance with less volatility. In the next step, Dow Jones constructed an index to track the six-stage model. The result is the systematically adjusted *Dow Jones Pring Business Cycle Index*, the first proactively managed business cycle index for Dow Jones. The index incorporates a rules-based system that identifies the six stages and optimizes allocations according to how each asset class and equity sector traditionally performed in every business cycle phase. *According to Dow Jones Indexes, the index has outperformed equities, bonds, commodities, and multiasset benchmarks on an absolute and risk-adjusted basis over the 1955–2012 time period.*

Index Construction Step 1: Identify the Stages

In order to identify the stages, the first step was to develop three models or barometers, one for each asset class: bonds, stocks, and commodities. Each barometer is constructed from a combination of trend-following, momentum, and interasset relationships. The prevailing stage of the business cycle is determined by the combination of these three barometers. For example, if the stock and commodity models are bullish and bonds are bearish, that would signify stage 4. If all three are bearish, stage 6 is indicated. Please refer once again to Table 8-2 in Chapter 8 for proper stage identification.

The barometer performance back to 1955 was confirmed by Dow Jones Indexes. The performance has been stress-tested under all kinds of geopolitical turmoil, wars, economic distress, and monetary conditions and embraces periods of inflation, deflation, crashes, booms, and busts. The return for each barometer is shown in Charts 9-1, 9-2, and 9-3, respectively.

The light highlights indicate when a specific barometer is bearish, the dark shade reflects bullish readings. On the PDF file on our website, bullish and bearish periods as defined by the barometers have been highlighted in green and red, respectively. The barometers were designed to identify significant financial market turning points as early in a new trend as possible. Arguably it is of greater importance to achieve consistency by trying to make sure that once a signal is triggered, it stays in force for at least four to six months. The vast majority of the time that does happen, but the real world is not as perfect as its theoretical counterpart. We are looking for an edge, not expecting perfection. The occasional one- and two-month whipsaw signal is unavoidable. It is always possible to construct special rules or introduce myriad indicators to fit the data and improve performance. However, since we are interested only in the past as a guide to the future, the more complicated a model design is the more likely it will

CHART 9-1 Pring Turner's Bond Barometer Performance, 1956–2011
The bond barometer defines favorable or unfavorable environments for bonds, and combined with other barometers defines the business cycle stage.

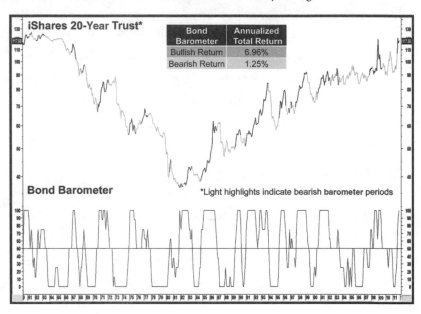

Source: Pring Turner Capital Group

fail in real time. Again it goes back to the desire to strive for consistency and timeliness rather than exactness.

The series in Chart 9-1 is the iShares Barclays 20-Year Trust ETF, with the symbol TLT. Since this bond ETF's history is fairly limited, it has been spliced to the price of a synthetic government 20-year constant maturity bond.

The barometer works very well most of the time and adds value by keeping you invested during favorable bond holding periods. An occasional misstep occurs; for example, when the market was bullish during the sharp early 2009 bond price drop and bearish during part of the 2011 rally.

The principal function of the stock barometer is to warn you about and enable you to avoid cyclical bear markets as much as possible. Chart 9-2 shows that, for the most part, it accurately warned of the vast majority of the bear markets since the 1950s. One drawback is that it is subject to some whipsaw signals as in the 1981–1982 bear market and a false bearish signal in 1965. Another incident occurred when it remained bullish during the 1987 crash. The reason is this isolated event was totally unrelated to business cycle developments. Our business cycle models assume that when markets turn, they usually do so in a relatively slow and deliberate fashion. Although not perfect, the stock barometer has a very credible long-term track record. The principal function of the stock barometer is to give you confidence and guide you to invest early during major advances. It is especially helpful during secular bear markets to warn you to stay out of major market declines, thus protecting your valuable assets.

CHART 9-2 **Pring Turner's Stock Barometer Performance, 1956–2011**
The stock barometer defines favorable or unfavorable environments for stocks, and combined with other barometers defines the business cycle stage.

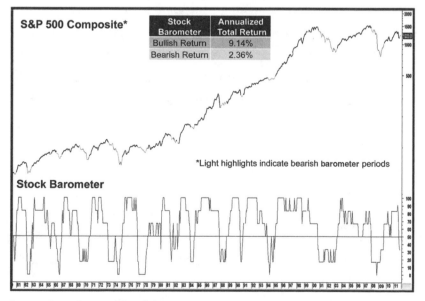

Source: Pring Turner Capital Group

CHART 9-3 Pring Turner's Inflation Barometer Performance, 1956–2011
The inflation barometer defines favorable or unfavorable environments for commodities, and combined with other barometers defines the business cycle stage.

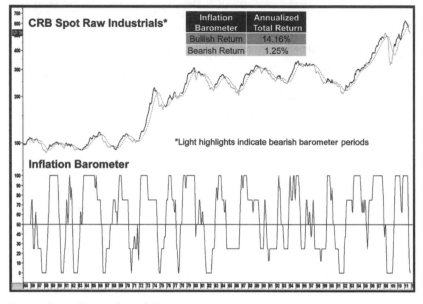

Source: Pring Turner Capital Group

Finally, the inflation barometer, which monitors commodity prices, is featured in Chart 9-3. We use the CRB Spot Raw Industrials as our benchmark. This index does not include any weather-driven commodities, except for cotton, and is therefore more sensitive to business cycle conditions than other commodity series. Because of its heavy industrial raw material weighting, the CRB Spot has a strong economic influence on inflation and interest rates.

The commodity model has correctly avoided the big declines but also has infrequent whipsaw signals, such as the bear period in 2005 and several bear periods in the mid-1990s. The inflation barometer has demonstrated clear added value to the asset allocation process over the course of many business cycles. The three barometers individually indicate a favorable or unfavorable holding period for each particular asset class. However, when combined, the barometers will signal a specific stage of the business cycle. This pattern or combination of the three barometers gives us six stages of a business cycle and demonstrate that markets are rational, logical, and sequential. In Chapter 6, these business cycle turning points are readily identified, and sequences are clearly demonstrated in the real world. Combining the three barometers is the basis for creating the Dow Jones Pring U.S. Business Cycle Index, a valuable road map to not only identify the business cycle stage but also indicate how to profitably allocate assets.

Index Construction Step 2: Asset Allocation by Stage
Once the stages have been identified through the combined status of the barometers, the next step is to assess how the individual asset classes perform in each stage. Using this proprietary performance information makes it possible to establish an allocation by asset class for each stage. For example, the average stage 2 is the most bullish one for stocks, less so for bonds, and usually one to avoid in the commodity arena. On the other hand bonds perform well in stage 1, but both stocks and commodities underperform in this stage, so assets would be rotated to reflect the situation depending on individual circumstances. In other words the portfolio would experience a very high bond allocation in stage 1 and a very low one in stage 5, when bonds underperform. For stocks the highest equity allocation would take place in stage 2 but this is less the case in stage 1, the initial phase of the cycle.

There are two other minor stages (7 and 8 discussed earlier) that are exceptions to our sequential business cycle model. These two outlier situations exist only about 10 percent of the time and are less significant but worth noting. The other 90 percent of the time the world does work in a rational, logical, and sequential manner, a definite edge for business cycle followers.

**Index Construction Step 3: Stock Market Sector
Allocation by Stage**

The final step the Dow Jones and Pring teams undertook was an assessment of the performance of individual stock markets by stage. For example, in stage 1 the stock market generally faces headwinds. A small equity allocation is justified in this early stage, but only in sectors that are sensitive or respond to a weak economy. A few select sectors such as consumer staples and utilities outperform because they are largely driven by falling interest rates. By the same token, Dow Jones Indexes found that healthcare stocks do well later in stage 5 when the overall market is vulnerable. It is therefore appropriate to include a healthcare allocation in the stage 5 allocation mix.

The Index and ETF

The end result of these three steps is the Dow Jones Pring Business Cycle Index. It is licensed by Dow Jones Indexes to institutional portfolio managers who might wish to allocate a portion of their assets under management to this business cycle approach. It could also serve as a basis for an ETF or mutual fund down the road. The history of the index, between 1956 and 2011, is featured in Chart 9-4. It is also carried by several data vendors under the symbol DJPRING. The symbol format depends on how the provider classifies the index, for example, Bloomberg (DJPRING:IND) and Yahoo! (^DJPRING).

Table 9-1 shows the overall performance by stage for both the 1956–2011 and 1994–2011 periods. It is certainly encouraging that the index offered a positive rate of return in every stage. However, it is also important to bear in mind that these are *average* numbers and that in some cycles the index did have drawdowns in a specific stage. For example the index declined by 10 percent in the 2000–2002 bear market and then took 8 months to recover to new highs. But that compared favorably to the S&P 500 drop of −50 percent in that bear

CHART 9-4 Dow Jones Pring U.S. Business Cycle Index Performance, 1956–2011

Using Pring Turner's barometer signals since 1956 to identify stages and actively allocate among bonds, stocks, and commodities, Dow Jones Indexes backtested the performance. They concluded there was solid value added with less volatility for investors following the index.

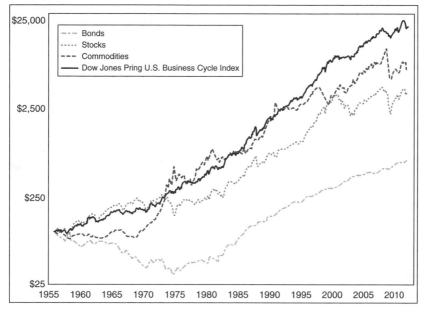

Source: Dow Jones Indexes

market, and as of early 2012, the S&P 500 Index has yet to recover to its old high. In the 2008 financial meltdown, the Dow Jones Pring Index loss was −19 percent with a 10-month recovery period. Again, compared to the S&P 500's −50 percent whipping, this was exceptional relative performance, while the S&P 500, as of early 2012, has yet to recover all of its lost ground. The Dow Jones Pring Business Cycle Index may well be a steadfast guide to help the Smiths survive and prosper as they invest in the second lost decade.

Note that there are two columns of results. One shows performance for 1956 through year-end 2011, and the other for 1994–2011. The reason two performance results are displayed is that some of the investment

TABLE 9-1 Dow Jones Pring Index Performance by Stage
The combination of dynamic asset allocation changes and effective sector rotation
throughout the business cycle resulted in positive returns in every stage (on average)
and impressive risk-adjusted returns. Note: Some individual stages experienced
negative returns and future results will vary.

Stage	Dow Jones Pring Index 1956–2011	Dow Jones Pring Index 1994–2011
1	7.8%	3.4%
2	15.0%	15.6%
3	18.3%	8.2%
4	8.5%	12.5%
5	7.8%	9.2%
6	9.7%	6.6%
7	4.3%	4.7%
8	4.5%	14.0%
Total	10.1%	11.2%

Source: Dow Jones Indexes

vehicles used in the index were not available to investors prior to 1994.
As an example, commodities in the longer time period reflect only the
CRB Spot Raw Industrials price index, whereas since 1994 investors
could actually invest in the Dow Jones-UBS Commodity Index via an
exchange-traded note (ETN), symbol DJP. See the website at www.
mhprofessional.com/mediacenter/ for additional historical data.

In view of the fact that data for some of the actual vehicles used in
the index have been available only since 1994, we end this chapter by
limiting our performance focus to 1994–2011. It is extremely important to note, of course, that there are no guarantees that the index
will be as profitable going forward as it was in the past. Bearing that
in mind, Chart 9-5 and Table 9-2 summarize the total return performance since 1994.

It is quite clear from the chart and the table that the index has outperformed all three asset classes in the 17-year period between 1994
and through 2011. Notice that the index not only outperformed stocks
and commodities, but it managed to do so with significantly lower

CHART 9-5 **Dow Jones Pring U.S. Business Cycle Index Performance, 1994–2011**

Since 1994, the Dow Jones Pring U.S. Business Cycle Index has outperformed all three asset classes while experiencing roughly two-thirds the risk (volatility) of the U.S. stock market.

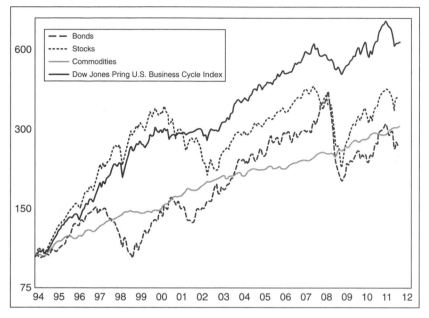

Source: Dow Jones Indexes

TABLE 9-2 **Dow Jones Pring U.S. Business Cycle Index Risk/Reward Versus Benchmark Asset Classes, 1994–2011 and 1956–2011**

The Dow Jones Pring Business Cycle Index outperformed each individual asset class over these two long-term time horizons.

Index Performance (1994–2011)				
Index	Bonds	Stocks	Commodities	Dow Jones Pring
Annualized Return	6.70%	8.26%	5.53%	11.25%
Standard Deviation	3.68%	16.20%	16.13%	10.83%
Index Performance (1956–2011)				
Index	Bonds	Stocks	Commodities	Dow Jones Pring
Annualized Return	3.44%	6.83%	7.95%	10.05%
Standard Deviation	6.81%	13.40%	15.10%	9.70%

Source: Dow Jones Indexes

risk. The standard deviation for the S&P was 16.2 percent, yet the standard deviation for the index was only 10.83 percent—the lower the standard deviation, the less the volatility and risk. Only the bond standard deviation was less than the index; however, the annualized return for the bonds was over 40 percent less than the performance of the Dow Jones Pring Index over the same time frame.

As you can see, the rotational nature of the business cycle allows the index to participate in those asset classes and sectors when they are putting in their best perormance and avoiding or down playing in the asset classes at those times when they have traditionally under-performed. Once again it is important to stress that the past is only a guide to the future and certainly no guarantee of similar profits going forward.

KEY POINTS

1. Dow Jones Indexes, a leading index research organization, analyzed Pring Turner's business cycle stage analysis and barometer signals since 1956 and confirmed the methodology works with favorable risk-adjusted results.
2. The proprietary barometer models are designed to determine cyclically bullish and bearish periods for stocks, bonds, and commodities.
3. The Dow Jones Index and Pring teams constructed an active index based on the barometer signals that dynamically adjusts asset allocation and sector emphasis around the six stages of the business cycle.
4. Investors can look forward to an actively managed, tactically allocated, "business cycle" ETF based on the Dow Jones Pring Business Cycle Index to become available late in 2012—subject to SEC approval.

IMPORTANT QUESTIONS FROM THE SMITHS

This sounds like market timing. All we have ever read on the subject says that this cannot be done successfully. What is the difference between this strategy and market timing?

There are quite a number of advisors utilizing so-called market-timing strategies; many are known as trend-followers, who more often than not are either all in or all out of any given market. Those utilizing trend-following strategies may make abrubt and exteme bets to "time" the markets in an effort to fully participate in up periods and be completely out in down markets. It is difficult for any manager to be consistently right and deliver on these objectives. In constrast, the business cycle approach is never all in or all out of any market. The six-stage method is really more about risk management and understanding the sequential nature of financial markets. Using history as a guide, it is possible to anticipate the favorable and unfavorable "seasons" for stocks, bonds, and commodities. Additionally, the historcial best- and worst-performing stock sectors for each stage can be identified to further reduce risk and improve the odds of success. Like any strategy, it is not perfect, so there are periods of both strong and weak performance. However, over the longer term, the results are rewarding both on a capital appreciation and risk-adjusted basis.

Another major difference between the index and market-timing strategies is that portfolio changes are made gradually and allocations are not taken to extremes (for instance, to be 100 percent cash). Instead, portfolio asset allocations are methodically increased or decreased based on the current stage analysis and historical risk and reward relationships. The result, as demonstrated by the Dow Jones Pring Business Cycle Index, is a very strong risk-adjusted performance without taking extreme bets to be in or out of the market at any given time.

Dow Jones Disclaimer

© CME Group Index Services LLC 2012. All rights reserved. "Dow Jones Indexes" is a licensed trademark of CME Group Index Services LLC ("CME Indexes"). "Dow Jones®," "Dow Jones Indexes," "DJ," "Dow Jones Pring U.S. Business Cycle Index," and all other index names listed above are service marks of Dow Jones Trademark Holdings, LLC ("Dow Jones") and have been licensed for use by CME Indexes. "CME" is a trademark of Chicago Mercantile Exchange Inc. "Pring" is a service mark of Pring Research. The Dow Jones Pring U.S. Business Cycle Index is published pursuant to an agreement between CME Indexes and Pring Research.

Investment products based on or represented in the Dow Jones Pring U.S. Business Cycle Index are not sponsored, endorsed, sold, or promoted by Dow Jones, CME Indexes, or their respective affiliates and none of Dow Jones, CME Indexes, or any of their respective affiliates make any representation regarding the advisability of investing in such products. Inclusion of a company or investment product in any of the indexes in these materials does not in any way reflect an opinion of Dow Jones, CME Indexes, or any of their respective affiliates on the investment merits of such company or investment product. None of Dow Jones, CME Indexes, or any of their respective affiliates is providing investment advice in connection with these indexes.

All information in these materials is provided "as is." CME Indexes, Dow Jones, and their respective affiliates do not make any representation regarding the accuracy or completeness of these materials, the content of which may change without notice, and each of CME Indexes, Dow Jones, and their respective affiliates disclaim liability related to these materials.

CHAPTER 10

PORTFOLIO RISK MANAGEMENT

Secular bear markets, with their deeply cyclical twists and turns, compel investors to be especially focused on careful risk management in portfolios. This critical overriding function is essential to surviving the second lost decade with both your assets and psyche intact. This chapter summarizes the layers of risk management that must be considered in order to successfully navigate this treacherous environment.

Judging Risk Versus Return

The secular outlook sets the big-picture framework for understanding the risks and opportunities in today's investment world. Secular bull markets are easy, as rising long-term trends act as a tailwind for portfolio performance. Mistakes are quickly forgiven as short-term market declines are eventually overshadowed by the major long-term uptrend. On the other hand, secular bears are more difficult as markets exhibit increased cyclicality and face strong headwinds. Investors who understand the increased difficulty of the long-term bearish environment should adopt focused tactical strategies to protect and grow capital during business cycle upturns. In this vein, recognizing and identifying secular and cyclical trends described in earlier chapters are an important first step. What other tactics can help investors manage risk through a challenging secular bear market? At Pring Turner Capital Group we employ a number of additional risk-management tactics to stabilize portfolio values and guard against heightened risk. Taken together these tactics not only deliver better results but also significantly improve an investor's peace of mind.

When evaluating a new investment, most investors ask, "How much money can I make?" This is only one question. The other is, "What are the downside risks, or how can this investment lose money?" Losses in investing are inevitable, but it is absolutely critical that you avoid big losses in your portfolio. This chapter demonstrates why managing risk is the key to your long-term investing success. We also introduce basic methods to better help you manage your own investment risks.

Risk Management and the "Law of Large Losses"

At the heart of your investment strategy should be careful risk management, which is a misused and underappreciated concept. At Pring Turner, we prefer to use the term "loss management" because *losing wealth* takes on a much more personal and deeper meaning than simply *managing risk*. Considering that stocks spend roughly one-third of the time in bear markets, the need to manage losses is imperative. In this current secular bear market, stock declines will continue to be deep and more frequent, thus the need for you to be even more aware of "loss management." It is an investment fact of life that bear markets exist on a regular basis, and more often than not the drops are a result of a change in business cycle activity. The Smiths began accumulating assets in their thirties and will continue to manage and depend on those investment assets to sustain their desired standard of living well into their eighties. This is a 50-plus-year

TABLE 10-1 Bear Markets Since 1960
Investors will suffer through many cyclical bear markets (−20% or more declines)
during their investment lifetime. The past 50 years included nine instances where the
Dow Jones Industrial Average experienced a significant decline (−33% on average).

Beginning Year	Duration (Months)	DJIA Decline
1961	6	−26%
1966	8	−25%
1968	17	−33%
1973	22	−45%
1976	17	−26%
1981	15	−23%
1987	2	−33%
2000	36	−34%
2007	16	−53%
Average	15.4	−33%

Source: Pring Turner Capital Group

process of investment management—not a sprint, but a marathon. How many bear markets can the Smiths expect to encounter in a 50-year investment horizon? Let's look at history as a guide for a window into the future (Table 10-1).

Investors today should plan on bear markets developing on a consistent basis. The past 50 years show the 9 instances (roughly every 5.5 years on average) that the Dow Jones Industrial Average experienced a significant bear market decline, with the average measuring −33 percent. One interesting side note is that 8 of the 9 business cycle–associated bear markets took place during an ongoing secular bear market.

These periodic bear markets are a real hazard to your wealth, and the "law of large losses" demonstrates the painful result from a portfolio suffering a large loss during a bear market. The law requires geometric (exponential) gains in your portfolio in order for you to recapture large losses. Do not worry if math is not your strong suit;

FIGURE 10-1 Law of Large Losses
The importance of not losing big: it is mathematically difficult to get back to even after suffering a large loss.

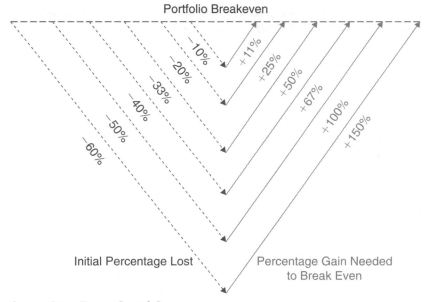

Source: Pring Turner Capital Group

a simple explanation appears in Figure 10-1. For example, a portfolio loss of 10 percent must be recouped with a gain of 11 percent. A larger decline of 33 percent requires a much more difficult 50 percent advance just to get back to even.

To put this into perspective, a buy-and-hold investor from late 2007 through early 2009 (market peak to trough) lost approximately 57 percent of his or her portfolio and would need a gain of 133 percent in order to break even. Needless to say, in a secular bear market it could take several years for the buy-and-hold investor to reach breakeven. Limiting losses is even more crucial for the Smiths' retirement because they depend on withdrawing portions of capital from their investment portfolio. Withdrawals impair gains and intensify losses, making it even more important to have consistent portfolio returns with minimal losses. Let us assume that the previously mentioned buy-and-hold investor is retired and withdraws 5 percent annually from his or her portfolio to pay for living expenses. What percentage gain does this investor need to recoup the 2007–2009 investment losses in addition to the withdrawals? Over 182 percent! When you combine our forecast for more frequent and deep stock market declines with the law of large losses, the average retiree's challenge becomes even more daunting. In fact, retirees are past the point of no return and will sadly outlive their nest eggs. Profitability and even survival is hugely dependent on playing a great game of stock market defense. As Warren Buffett says simply, "An investor needs to do very few things right as long as he or she avoids big mistakes."

Defense is the tactical approach for protecting your hard-earned assets, and there are multiple approaches to help you accomplish this goal. The process of protecting assets can be likened to the multiple-layer structure of an onion. The best defense incorporates many layers of risk protection in order to effectively reduce volatility and protect against large losses. The more layers, the better your portfolio is protected, and the better you sleep at night. So let's bring the Smiths into the real world of loss management. What can they do during the rest of this secular bear market to preserve and build capital? The key building blocks every investor should incorporate are: tactical asset allocation, diversification, quality, value, and income.

The Critical Role of Tactical Asset Allocation

The most essential determinant of the Smiths' ultimate success is how they allocate investments among asset classes. In earlier chapters we thoroughly explained the rationale for a secular bear market in stocks and bonds. We also introduced the business cycle and how the main asset classes typically behave in a rational, logical, and sequential manner around a business cycle. This knowledge is the framework for generating better returns with less risk. The Smiths can manage it by gradually adjusting portfolio allocations and emphasizing the right sectors depending on where they are in the business cycle.

Another important risk-management layer is paying attention to intermediate market moves—moves in the market that last any- where from two to six months and can take prices up or down by at least 10 percent. The "market cycle model" (Figure 10-2) shows our familiar bell-shaped curve of the typical four- to five-year cycle revolving around economic expansion and contraction periods.

We all know that the market does not move this smoothly. Fluctuat- ing above and below the major cycle trend are the intermediate-term

FIGURE 10-2 Market Cycle Model
Intermediate market moves o ffer investors additional profit opportunities to plant or prune investments within the business cycle trend.

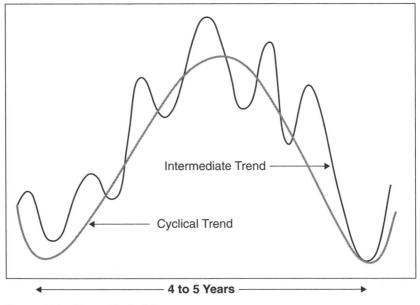

Source: Pring Turner Capital Group

moves (of two to six months duration) that offer investors additional profit opportunities to plant or prune investments within the cyclical trend. To identify these intermediate moves, we use a comprehensive form of market analysis. This form of analysis involves measuring three key components that directly affect stock prices: *monetary conditions, trend work,* and *investor sentiment.*

Monetary Conditions

Monetary conditions refer to whether the Federal Reserve's monetary policy is tight (bad) or loose (good). How can you know whether monetary policy is tight or loose? The Fed's job is to fight either inflation or unemployment. If unemployment is running high, the Fed will run a loose money policy. If inflation is running high, the Fed will be combating that with a tight money policy. A simple reading of the FOMC (Federal Open Market Committee) meeting notes released every six weeks will reveal the Fed's overriding concerns and monetary direction. The Federal Reserve utilizes many different tools to exercise monetary policy, including setting the discount rate, margin requirements, and bank reserve requirements. In total, its policy does have a powerful impact on the economy and financial markets.

Trend Work

A good doctor takes blood pressure, pulse, and other vital signs to gauge a patient's health. Trend work is the measure of the "internal" health of the market. The internal health of the market is measured by such indicators as advancing versus declining stocks, new highs versus new lows, up to down volume, and others. Trend work also measures whether the stock market is overstretched to the upside (overbought) or to the downside (oversold) and most likely poised to rebound in the other direction. This rebound is also termed "regression to the mean." Observing and making small portfolio adjustments based on these two- to six-month intermediate price swings can be profitable and incrementally add to performance.

Investor Sentiment

Investment psychology is best used as a contrary indicator that tracks whether investors are overly fearful (good) or greedy (bad). The easiest of the three market analysis areas to quickly understand is investor psychology, since we are all human and subject to the same emotional tendencies. Indeed, a good understanding of your own emotions and how they affect portfolio decision making can be the difference between investment success or failure. The "investor sentiment cycle" (Figure 10-3) shows the typical range and sequence of feelings that often take investors from one emotional extreme to the other.

FIGURE 10-3 Investor Sentiment Cycle
Gauging investor psychology is one way for investors to identify intermediate and cyclical market turning points.

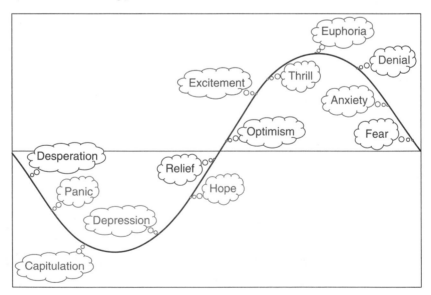

Source: Dow Jones Indexes

Any seasoned investor is sure to recognize these familiar feelings that come into play as markets gyrate back and forth. We have been portfolio managers working in the business over many cycles, and it is amazing to observe just how quickly market emotions change. Measuring these mood swings is critical to effectively navigate the intermediate market moves. It is helpful for us to understand these emotional extremes in an effort to protect ourselves from ourselves— from our own emotions.

One easy way to understand investment psychology is to analyze two recent sharp intermediate-term market declines. These serve as good examples of regression to the mean and shifting investor sentiment that create intermediate market moves. Near 20 percent declines in the middle of the recent cyclical bull market from May 2010 to July 2010 and another from July 2011 to October 2011 are ideal learning examples. Why did the market decline by nearly 20 percent in a short few months? Did the economy or GDP pull back by 20 percent? No. Did unemployment climb rapidly? No. Did retail sales plunge or inflation jump by double digits? No. Did corporate earnings per share collapse abruptly? No. What did change? Investor sentiment changed. Investor psychology swung from being too optimistic about economic conditions to being overly pessimistic. The market cycle model diagram (Figure 10-2) captures the essence of these intermediate trends. Investor emotional swings create profitable intermediate opportunities for astute observers.

The point of this book is not to go into great detail on any of these market analysis topics but to introduce the concept as another layer of risk management. For more complete details you can refer to Martin Pring's longtime bestseller *Technical Analysis Explained* (McGraw-Hill, 2002). This detailed textbook is required reading in order for professionals to receive the chartered market technician (CMT) designation and includes ample material on all facets of market analysis.

Quality Counts

The Smiths can sleep better at night if they emphasize stocks and bonds of high-quality-rated companies. Through many decades of financial studies, a common investment theme continues to emerge: the higher the quality, the better the performance on a risk-adjusted basis. Unfortunately in reality, selecting quality investments is easier said than done because this is a highly subjective process. Beauty, or in this case quality, is in the eye of the beholder. So what are telltale characteristics to look for in a high-quality company? A high-quality company is able to consistently grow earnings over the long term regardless of the underlying business atmosphere. Corporations have witnessed their fair share of economic complications in the opening decade of the twenty-first century, and the highest-quality companies were well prepared for this treacherous environment. They came through the post–2009 period in strong financial standing, with many even thriving.

Now that we have defined a high-quality company, let us revisit the question; what are the common characteristics found in these companies? A primary characteristic of a quality company is one that demonstrates a sustainable competitive advantage in a promising industry, allowing for increased earning potential without threat of new rivals. Microsoft provides a good example of a company with a sustainable competitive advantage against its peers as it maintains a stranglehold on the PC, server, and video-gaming markets. Since the turn of the century, Microsoft has steadily grown revenue and earnings per share over fourfold. This clearly is an enviable record of revenue and earnings growth. However, the Smiths are wondering why Microsoft was one of the worst performers in their retirement account over the same time period. Let's put that issue on hold for now; we will answer it in the forthcoming section on value. First let's discuss other key determinants of quality: management and operating performance.

Corporate management is often overlooked by individual investors, but it should not be. Management teams devoted to the long-term profitability of shareholders (instead of the short-term profitability of their personal investment accounts) are especially important. One way to identify management teams that are closely aligned with shareholders is to check the teams' exposure to the company stock. Executives holding a high percentage of their personal net worth in company stock will be motivated for shareholders' long-term success. This alone does not ensure investment success, but it is reassuring for investors to know that corporate managers have a direct vested interest in shareholder success.

High-quality companies typically possess key common operational features found in their financial statements. Maintaining strong free cash flows is one essential feature high-quality businesses share. Free cash flow is the extra cash left over after a company pays all its operating expenses. An easy way to understand this concept is to relate cash flow from a personal perspective. For example, during your working career, you collect a paycheck every two weeks that is "all yours to spend." Unfortunately, we know this is not entirely true because much of your paycheck has already been spent on mortgage/rent, utilities, food, transportation, insurance, healthcare, and taxes. After paying off all these costs of living, you are now free to spend the remaining funds on anything you desire. This is your personal free cash flow. It works the same way for corporations. Greater free cash flows in your personal life leads to higher personal freedom, and greater free cash flows in a corporation lead to higher corporate freedom. Freedom is always a good thing, especially in the business world. A substantial free cash flow allows companies to finance themselves internally, which makes them relatively independent from the business cycle. This is especially important in times of economic hardship, as credit and financial markets weaken. For example, smart corporate managers are in a position to take advantage of bargains being offered in the marketplace during hard times through the initiation of stock buybacks. Purchases of other businesses and hiring of new talent represent additional opportunities.

Recurring revenue and low debt levels are operational features that round out the characteristics to be found in high-quality businesses.

It is a distinct advantage to have repeat business year after year. Recurring revenue streams provide a safety zone and allow the company to focus on growing its business. Take the Coca-Cola Company for example, in which a majority of its customers (restaurants, wholesalers, and supermarkets) need to buy Coke products on a continual basis. This takes pressure off of Coca-Cola operationally because it allows management to more accurately forecast future demand and lets the sales team focus on acquiring new revenue pipelines. In contrast, companies that provide discretionary big-ticket items such as automobiles, housing, vacation packages, and luxury goods do not share this continuous and significant revenue stream. Cyclically sensitive companies carry more operational risk as they are more susceptible to changes in consumer confidence and spending patterns during the ups and downs of the business cycle. When there is nothing but blue economic skies, consumers have confidence to purchase big-ticket items such as a house, a new automobile, or an international vacation. But as economic storm clouds start to gather, optimism can fade quickly. Consumers tighten their purse strings, and the first items they tend to cut out are those big-ticket discretionary purchases. Owning high-quality companies with recurring business, not dependent on the level of economic activity or the level of consumer confidence, is a great way to reduce investment risks.

The quality status of corporations can also be determined by their use of debt. Debt is a double-edged sword; it intensifies profits and exacerbates losses. If used prudently, debt can provide operational, financial, and tax benefits to a company. By maintaining relatively low debt levels, a company retains its freedom to make mistakes without sustaining catastrophic repercussions. However, the use of debt can be a slippery slope. Reckless management teams will eventually rely on excessive leverage to maintain their corporate profitability. Investors would be wise to stay far away from these heavily debt-laden organizations. Ultimately, it is best to invest in companies that rely on sound business principles to generate profits, not ones that rely on debt. Warren Buffett said it best in his 1990 annual shareholder newsletter:

> Huge debt, we were told, would cause operating managers to focus their efforts as never before, much as a dagger mounted on the steering wheel of a car could be expected to make its driver proceed with intensified care. We'll acknowledge that such an attention-getter would produce a very alert driver. But another certain consequence would be a deadly—and unnecessary— accident if the car hit even the tiniest pothole or sliver of ice. The roads of business are riddled with potholes; a plan that requires dodging them all is a plan for disaster.

Conservatively managed companies will occasionally hit a financial bump in the road, but they are not likely to run off the road and crash because of one bump.

A number of academic studies prove that exceptionally well-managed global companies in leadership positions tend to have better earnings and dividend stability and are less likely to surprise investors with unfavorable news than less well-managed companies. Since 1956 Standard & Poor's has published quality rankings and researched company performance over many years. The ratings reflect an analysis of the 10-year record of earnings and dividend growth and stability with financial strength. The S&P ratings reflect the relative quality of major corporations and provide a simple method for focusing or screening quality stocks. This information is widely available through many brokerage sites or community libraries that have access to S&P research reports. In October 2005 Standard & Poor's reported that: (1) portfolios of stocks with high quality rankings outperformed the S&P 500 Index and substantially outperformed portfolios of stocks with low quality rankings over the 1986–2004 period, (2) portfolio risk is lower in portfolios of stocks with high quality rankings, (3) fundamental risk (business risk) is lower in portfolios of stocks with high quality rankings, (4) portfolios of stocks with high quality rankings provide downside protection in times of earnings deceleration and increasing credit risk, and (5) earnings growth for companies with high quality rankings are not correlated with overall corporate earnings and credit cycles. Table 10-2 compares the performance of a portfolio of stocks containing companies rated A, B, C, and D with the performance of the S&P 500.

The data support investing in high-quality companies to increase portfolio returns while reducing volatility. The lower risk characteristics of a high-quality portfolio are especially appreciated in a secular bear market where defending your investment portfolio from significant

TABLE 10-2 1986–2004: Annual Returns for Standard & Poor's Quality Rankings
Standard & Poor's has demonstrated over the long run that higher-quality companies outperform lower-quality companies with less risk (volatility).

	A Rated	B Rated	C & D Rated	S&P 500
Annual Return	13.10%	11.80%	9.30%	12.30%
Standard Deviation	14.70%	18.10%	29.30%	15.60%
Return/Risk	0.89	0.65	0.32	0.79
Beta	0.87	1.07	1.37	1

Source: Standard & Poor's Quality Rankings: Portfolio Performance, Risk, and Fundamental Analysis

losses is most crucial. While having the highest-quality investments in your portfolio is certainly desirable, this alone does not guarantee success. Equally important is your ability to purchase these investments at bargain prices.

The Long-Term Appeal of Value Investing

"Price is what you pay. Value is what you get." These are the astute words of Benjamin Graham, who is considered by many to be the first proponent of value investing. Graham believed the key to successful investing was to purchase shares of good businesses when market prices were trading at a large discount relative to their underlying value. He coined the term "margin of safety" to describe the discounted price paid for a security. By purchasing investments with a margin of safety, investors stack another layer of risk management onto their portfolios. Indeed Mr. Smith had purchased a high-quality company—Microsoft. However the price he paid was too large a premium to underlying value. Mr. Smith lacked a "margin of safety," and this is the reason for the poor performance of this security in his retirement account.

Chart 10-1 plots Microsoft's performance and valuation covering 1995 to 2011. Microsoft's share price (adjusted for dividends and splits) is shown in the top third of the chart. Like countless technology stocks during 1995–2000, the stock exhibited exponential growth, skyrocketing from $5 to over $45, dramatically raising shareholders' future expectations. However, a major course correction has taken place since the inception of the secular bear market in 2000. Between 2000 and 2011 the stock has spent a majority of its time gyrating between the $20 and $30 levels which has frustrated the Smiths who believed that this high-quality company was a sure growth investment. In reality, Microsoft has actually lived up to its billing. The company has steadily grown earnings from $0.15 per share in 1995 to over $2.50 per share in

CHART 10-1 Microsoft's Performance and Valuation, 1995–2011

Like the overall stock market, Microsoft started the century at an extremely high valuation level. The combination of Microsoft's steady earnings growth and stagnant stock price has returned this high-quality company to a more attractive valuation level.

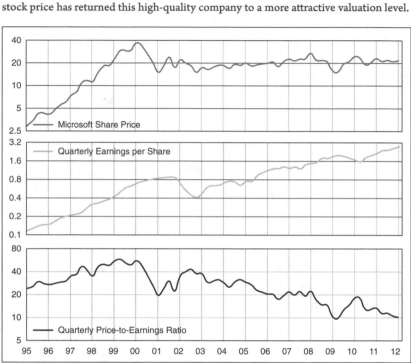

Source: Pring Turner Capital Group

2011 (shown in the middle of Chart 10-1). So what explains the poor stock performance? In a word, valuation. The downtrend of the price-to-earnings ratio depicted in the bottom third of Chart 10-1 illustrates Microsoft's journey from excessive overvaluation to undervaluation. At the height of the late 1990s, technology bubble investors were eager to purchase $1 of Microsoft earnings for $68.50 (P/E ratio of 68.5), while today weary investors are paying only $9.50 for that same $1 of earnings (P/E ratio of 9.5). Ultimately this P/E compression eroded all the growth in Microsoft's earnings and led to disappointing price performance for the Smiths. As discussed in our secular stock market outlook, this is not an isolated occurrence for Microsoft shareholders, as the broad stock market has also experienced this steady erosion of the price/earnings ratio.

Throughout the entirety of the secular bear market, companies will continue to become cheaper and cheaper. Purchasing stocks of high-quality companies *at attractive valuation levels* will limit the negative effect of valuation compression.

History demonstrates that this is not only successful but that it provides less volatility in investment portfolios. In his popular investment book *What Works on Wall Street* (McGraw-Hill, 2011), James O'Shaughnessy found:

> Your chances of beating [the stock market] with low P/E stocks in any 5-year period are 92 percent. . . . When we extend our odds to all rolling 10-year periods, we see that historically, low P/E stocks almost always beat [the stock market]. There are only 3 ten-year periods out of 433 in which low P/E stocks failed to beat the All Stocks universe. All the low P/E groups provided higher returns over the periods, with lower risk than that of the universe.

Although value investing may not have the allure and excitement of growth investing, this proves, in the long run, value investing out-performs growth investing with significantly less risk. There are a multitude of fundamental analysis sources that screen and measure securities for value characteristics. These valuation yardsticks add another layer of risk or loss management to portfolios.

The Role of Portfolio Income as a Shock Absorber

Like the majority of other investors, the Smiths' investment decision making focuses predominately on capital appreciation. This is a natural tendency because during a secular bull market the most spectacular gains are always achieved with capital appreciation. Income typically takes a backseat and in most cases gets little to no consideration at all. Unfortunately, the Smiths are missing out on the compounding factor of income that is a significant contributor to positive long-term portfolio performance, especially during a secular bear market. Income compounding becomes especially effective when it takes place over a long investment horizon. Investing for income lacks the appeal and excitement of growth-oriented investing, but it works. Companies that have historically produced sustained revenue and earnings growth pay regular dividends. They are generally well managed and in better financial health than the average non-dividend-paying company. Therefore a gradually rising dividend stream is a valuable aid to investors looking for current income but also concerned about keeping up with inflation.

Many people associate the term *compounding* with interest earned on principal and accumulated interest reinvested from prior periods that accompany fixed income investments. Compounding can also be accomplished with common stock dividends. In many instances dividend payments are periodically increased. There is a select universe of blue chip corporations called *dividend achievers*. This group has a history of increasing regular annual dividends. Another elite group has a proven record of enhancing shareholder value through increased dividend payouts for at least 25 years; these are termed *dividend aristocrats*. This blue chip roster with years of consecutive dividend hikes includes the likes of Abbott Laboratories (39), Kimberly-Clark (39), Johnson & Johnson (49), and Procter & Gamble (54). These aristocrats rewarded patient shareholders through any number of recessions, wars, oil price shocks, and banking crises.

Based on our secular inflation outlook, a gradually rising dividend stream will come in handy for portfolios. Consistent income serves as a stabilizing cushion for your investment portfolio, and quality dividends are a shock absorber when markets drop. Prices will always go up and down, but dependable income helps provide consistent performance with less volatility. Since 1900, income generated from dividends has contributed nearly half the total return of stock investments. The historical evidence demonstrates that during past secular bear markets investors received almost no profits from price gains in stocks. Instead, almost all of the total returns were generated from dividends. By combining reasonable income with high quality, value investments tactically allocated around the business cycle, investors can dramatically increase their probabilities of improved performance above and beyond just dividends.

A Comprehensive Risk-Management Process
The key for the Smiths is to incorporate all these techniques into their portfolio as each technique adds another layer of risk protection. The entire top-down portfolio management process we describe can be seen in the Figure 10-4.

It begins with understanding the secular environment for stocks, bonds, and commodities or inflation-sensitive assets. Then, when the business cycle stage calls for more defensive measures, the job for the portfolio manager is to change allocations and raise more cash, increase portfolio quality, and increase the income level of the securities in the portfolio. These tactics will keep portfolio losses to a minimum and allow investors to achieve new benchmark high levels in their wealth early into the next cyclical bull market. Remember, after each cyclical bear period another business cycle–associated bull market is on the horizon. Table 10-1 detailed the major cyclical bear markets in the Dow Jones average since 1960. Now study Table 10-3, which shows the ensuing bull markets that followed each bear.

FIGURE 10-4 Portfolio Management Process
To be successful in the second "lost decade," investors should incorporate many layers of risk management to safely build their portfolio.

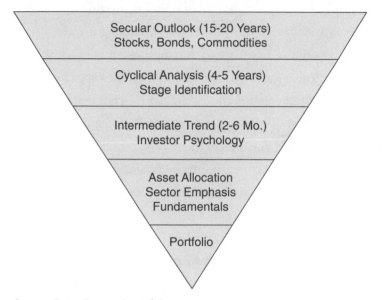

Source: Pring Turner Capital Group

TABLE 10-3 Bull Markets Since 1960
Each cyclical bear market is followed by profitable cyclical bull periods. The key to success is to carefully protect portfolios from large losses during cyclical declines and capitalize on ensuing bull markets.

Beginning Year	Duration (Months)	DJIA Advance
1962	42	83%
1966	25	32%
1970	30	58%
1974	21	75%
1978	36	37%
1982	60	237%
1987	29	66%
2003	53	82%
2009	?	?
Average	37	84%

Source: Pring Turner Capital Group

Certainly there will be cyclical opportunities to go on offense and grow wealth. Allocations to equity investments should be increased and tactical shifts into cyclical industries and emerging markets made. This allows investors to take full advantage of the extended "growing season."

The job to protect and grow wealth is a challenging task, but "loss management" is critical in navigating this secular bear market. We have introduced the absolute need and importance for the Smiths to first analyze risks. Second, to survive and even prosper in the years ahead, they need to incorporate many layers of defense into their decision-making process. Having a game plan to play great defense will increase their odds of not suffering big losses during the next cyclical bear market. The Smiths will then be in position to easily achieve new high levels of wealth during the ensuing cyclical bull market. The most important message to take away from this chapter is that in a secular bear market environment, all efforts are made to first protect capital.

KEY POINTS

1. Secular bear markets are inherently fraught with high risk, so loss management disciplines are especially important.
2. The "law of large losses" demonstrates the mathematical truism of the difficulty in just getting even, as the size of a loss increases. It highlights the importance of not losing big in the first place.
3. Tactical asset allocation around the normal sequences of the business cycle is an invaluable tool to reduce risk and improve performance.
4. Additional layers of risk management include careful attention to security quality, value gauges, and adding income from interest and dividends for boosting total portfolio returns.
5. The risk-management tactics outlined in this chapter will temper portfolio declines and smooth out the journey for conservative investors in the second lost decade.

IMPORTANT QUESTIONS FROM THE SMITHS

What about the simple but important "loss management" techniques such as diversification or stop-loss orders?

That is an important question, which begs a whole other subject of portfolio management tactics. We could write another book on elements of tactics, or what professionals refer to as a trading plan, that do include diversification, noncorrelation of assets, order entry or stalking a trade, stop-loss or aborting trades, and sector and position sizing, to name a few considerations of a trading plan. It is most important to have a well-thought-out trading plan for long-term investment success; however, it is beyond the scope of this chapter.

CHAPTER 11

DO IT YOURSELF OR HIRE A MONEY MANAGER?

For the Smiths the chore of investing their own portfolio has become significantly more difficult as the secular bear market environment plays out. What a stark contrast to the conditions they faced when the year 2000 rolled around. They fondly remember back to the late 1990s, as the prior 18-year secular bull market roared ahead in full glory. Their mutual fund holdings steadily built wealth and required little attention. That period climaxed with an incredible explosion of do-it-yourself day traders entering the investment world just when the online trading frenzy kicked into high gear. Encouraged by their seemingly effortless ability to pick winning stocks (virtually anything related to technology was in the midst of a parabolic climb higher), this new breed of speculator actually believed it was *easy* to compound investment profits of 20 percent or more annually.

Indeed, many people left their lucrative professional careers behind to trade the stock market, especially the technology and telecom darlings. Why in the world would they consider turning over the management of their portfolio to someone else (and pay fees) when they were making so much easy money and having such fun doing it themselves? But their temporary investment success was more a reflection on the age-old adage, "Never confuse brains with a roaring bull market." Almost a dozen years later, after a three-year 80 percent–plus decline in the Nasdaq from 2000 to 2003, followed by another 60 percent–plus decline in the overall market in 2008 and 2009, that do-it-yourself investment psychology had taken a 180-degree turn. The Smiths never joined the aggressive trading crowd; their conservative, go-slow approach was more fitting with their temperament. But now, after realizing that during the last 10 years the passive buy-and-hold approach produced less-than-adequate returns and plenty of uncertainty, the Smiths are seeking professional guidance. They ask, "How in the world are we supposed to manage our own portfolio in these volatile times?" Portfolio management certainly has not been easy lately and not as much fun for the individual investor either.

As secular trends change, individual investors' attitudes change with them. What happened in the late 1990s is not much different from investor behavior in the late 1920s or late 1960s, as those secular bulls peaked and gave way to new secular bears. The buying stampede was in full swing as those secular bull markets reached their peaks. Some argue that we have never seen an environment like today's, and we would disagree. It's just that these long-term trend changes don't come around very often. And when they do, the typical investor is just not prepared for them. It is pretty easy to understand why. Just as investors learn the rules of how to make money in a secular bull market (just buy and hang on), the rules of the game change. How unfortunate. Precisely when most participants have figured out how easy investing can be, a cruel reality sets in. They are still playing with the tactics that worked so well in a long-term bull market, but in the new deeply cyclical secular bear environment, they need to change their strategy. It takes time to first understand that you are playing a new ballgame, and then to learn the new set of rules to win.

Protecting Yourself from Yourself

Countless studies (for instance, by Dalbar) over the years have demonstrated the difference between an investment return (say a particular mutual funds' performance) and the average return the investor earns within the fund. Put another way, a mutual fund may have a great long-term track record based on the original dollar invested on day one. Unfortunately, investors recognize a fund only after it has outperformed for a considerable time. Such a fund attracts the most assets as it gains in popularity. So the average dollar invested in the fund earns a significantly different return (and often lower) from the original dollar invested. This is a subtle yet incredibly important distinction to make. How many investors purchased a highly ranked fund with a good track record only to be disappointed in its performance a few years later?

Many investors chase past-performance results and consequently invest *after* a fund has demonstrated success. Often that is late in the game for that fund's style, manager, sector, or asset class. Indeed, we could go on to say that the biggest mistake investors make is to invest when they "feel" good about a particular investment, discover a fund that has a good track record, and join the crowd as the investment's popularity climbs. And why wouldn't an investor feel good about that? The investment is being repeatedly mentioned favorably in the media, everyone else is buying it, overall the news background is good, and perhaps even a third-party research organization or newsletter is rating it highly. There is significant comfort in following the crowd which often validates the decision and makes it easy to justify. After all, if everyone else is recommending it, it must be good. That may work sometimes or for a short period, but very often investments disappoint the most soon after their popularity peaks. Precisely when asset levels reach their peak, a fund begins a significant period of underperformance. That was true of the vaunted Fidelity

Magellan Fund (or any other popular stock fund at the time; Magellan happened to be the largest) in the year 2000. For the next 10 years performance did not live up to the expectations of investors looking back at the stellar 10- and 20-year performance history. Gobs of money poured into the fund in the 1990s, especially as it neared its price peak.

That story helps explain why the average fund performance is often much different from the average dollar invested in the fund. Since most money came in near the top, most investors were disappointed with performance three years, five years, and ten years thereafter. The point of this discussion is not to disparage mutual fund managers; they know full well that money flows in and out of their funds based on past performance, and they are keenly focused on performance. Our point is that many investors need to protect themselves from themselves. There is a tendency for investors to let emotions drive their decision making and chase past performance. In this example, the emotion was greed, or the desire to find the "best" fund, or the "best" manager with the "best" return history. This typically translates into purchasing a fund after it has done very well for a considerable period of time and when there are plenty of fans recommending it.

Contrast the comfortable feeling in buying a highly rated fund to another one that has perhaps been an underperformer and offers good value, but is not highly touted. It takes a lot of courage to go against the crowd and purchase a new potential emerging winner before it is widely recognized and becomes a popular choice. No doubt, investing is a very emotional process and investors need to be aware of their own strengths and weaknesses. Investors must evaluate whether their emotions are a handicap to making successful investment decisions, like most investors, as reported in Dalbar studies, that buy high and sell low. In addition, investors must ask themselves: "Do I want to pay the 'tuition' necessary to become a good decision maker?" Another question to ask is: "Do I want to spend the time each day handling the responsibilities of this full-time job?"

The Smiths, like many investors, have to consider and decide whether they have the time, knowledge, experience, and, perhaps most important, emotional fortitude to do it on their own successfully. In the Smiths' case, after careful evaluation they concluded that by turning over the day-to-day duties of money management, they could better enjoy their retirement years and have greater peace of mind. The next step is to hire a professional money manager whose philosophy is compatible with their own needs. Their responsibility shifts from daily decision making to periodic oversight of the manager to ensure adherence to their objectives and to monitor performance. What are the considerations and questions the Smiths should ask as they evaluate financial professionals?

Finding the Right Money Manager for You

The most important thing for you to do when you're selecting a money manager to handle your portfolio is to fully explain your investment objectives and, as best you can, your ability to tolerate risk. Explaining your past experiences, both good and bad, is another important consideration that helps the advisor understand your circumstances and emotional makeup. Have you generally had success or disappointment when dealing with your investments? Why have they been positive or negative? What are your account balances, savings goals, retirement goals, and rate-of-return expectations? Based on your own beliefs and circumstances in these areas, are your long-term goals realistic or not? A good starting point for any interview is a frank discussion relating to your ability to tolerate risk. The agreed-upon level of risk tolerance puts a cap on the realistic expected total return. Once your tolerance for risk is established, the appropriate return commensurate with that risk can be calculated from historical data.

Now you and the advisor can judge whether the firm's investment philosophy and historic return ranges are consistent with your own objectives and risk tolerances. In other words, is there a realistic match so that the advisor will be able to deliver the stated return objectives while keeping risk levels within your comfort zone?

The next step is to fully understand the investment philosophy and decision-making process of the manager. Ask good questions. Can the manager clearly explain his strategy and how long he has been devoted to it? Does the strategy make sense to you? How does the manager go about protecting your portfolio during periodic cyclical bear markets? Specifically, how did the manager perform during the two 50 percent-plus market declines over the 2000–2011 time frame? Has the manager's performance been calculated using Global Investment Performance Standards (GIPS), the financial industry's standard used for measuring investment management performance, which can also be used to compare managers. How does the manager communicate with clients? How often and what type of educational information is provided to keep clients informed? Has the performance been consistent, and is it repeatable? Or could the good results be just a stretch of pure dumb luck? How long has the portfolio team been managing assets following this philosophy?

On Being a Good Client

Investment management clients focus on the manager's responsibility to them and their portfolio. But a client also has responsibilities to the manager. If you find that your objectives are consistent with the investment manager's philosophy, it is important to fully accept the broad concepts. If you say you agree with the strategy and sign a contract to engage the firm even though you do not fully accept the decision-making process, conflicts are sure to arise. For example, if the manager has a conservative approach and regards the protection of principal as the key objective for the portfolio, you may become frustrated at the overly safe strategy if riskier asset classes begin to take off. You may read about the great gains being made in a specific market sector or part of the world and may be disappointed that you are not participating in that market. The manager cannot be faulted for sticking with the firm's own philosophy that has served it and its clients well for years. This type of conflict between client and manager is a recipe for trouble. Only by fully buying in to the firm's investment strategy and making a commitment to stay the course will the relationship have a chance of success.

Even though managers hate to turn away prospective clients, it is in their and your long-term best interests for managers to indicate that you should look for another firm if your philosophies and risk-tolerance levels are not a good match. An unhappy client will leave sooner or later anyway, and difficult client relationships can drain money managers of the energy and time they need to devote to the markets and their other clients. Likewise, if you find that the manager is not performing up to your expectations or does not communicate clearly the direction he is taking the portfolio, it is best to search for a manager who is a better fit for your needs.

Assuming that you do have a good match with a successful money management firm, there are other important considerations that will make it a positive long-term relationship. Another imperative activity is keeping an open line of communication and dealing with the constant changes in emotions as markets swing back and forth. When a manager begins a relationship with a new client, he faces more than the battle of balancing risk versus reward and generating consistent performance. This is where the clients' responsibility steps in, which is to not let their emotions of fear and greed interfere with the manager's decision making.

The client places assets under management with a professional because he does not have the time, expertise, experience, or emotional aptitude to invest successfully for himself. The manager will often be investing in a manner that goes against the crowd. He will be buying when news is bad and selling when news is good. If the client doesn't have extensive market experience or an understanding of market relationships, he will likely be of the opposite emotional state. When prices decline, the news background is invariably negative. Keep in mind that the definition of a stock market bottom is the point of maximum pessimism. It is little wonder that we find the client calling up the manager when he has just made some purchases at fairly depressed levels. Similarly at the other extreme near market peaks, the manager may be selling some winning holdings to nail down profits, but the client may be second-guessing the decision to sell when the news flow is so good. Again, a stock market top is defined as the point of maximum optimism—truly a good time to sell. It is best to not interfere with a manager's decision-making process; you only damage yourself. In fact, successful portfolio managers measure investor psychology in order to take advantage of price extremes exaggerated by investor emotions of fear and greed. One investor's emotional crisis is another investor's low-risk opportunity.

Once you have rigorously examined the manager's methodology, performance, and so on and made the decision to have him handle your account, the best thing you can do for both of you is to let him alone to get on with his job. Avoid the temptation to interfere unnecessarily. Obviously, this does not mean that you cannot or should not periodically evaluate his performance, but you do need to give him the benefit of the doubt until enough time has gone by for you to be able to make an absolute judgment.

If the investment firm does not perform well for you after a period of two years or so, it may be time to reassess your relationship. It may be that the investment strategy is still relevant, but it has produced below-average returns over the past two years. This can happen to the best of investment approaches and is a simple fact of life. As long as there is no style drift (where the investment strategy changes demonstrably in an effort to catch up to the market), rough patches should be relatively short-lived. One thing a client can do before signing on with an investment firm is check the performance history of the advisor and study the results during the worst market periods. How did the manager do in comparison? Where are the slumps when the manager underperformed? How long did these weak periods last and how much time did it take for performance to get back on track? Good managers are able to successfully take portfolio valuations back to new all-time highs within a reasonable period of time. That type of information is invaluable for new clients especially as they endeavor to get through the inevitable rough stretches comfortably.

KEY POINTS

1. Secular bear markets are difficult for investors, and a simple buy-and-hold approach is frustrating and not very rewarding.
2. Individual investors need to be aware of how their emotions can interfere with the portfolio management process—that is, emotions play a critical role in portfolio performance.
3. Hiring a professional money manager is a suitable solution if you are not confident in your own abilities.
4. The more you allow the manager to do his job unencumbered the better his performance is likely to be.
5. Interviewing and finding the right professional who is a good match with your needs is possible if you ask the right questions.

IMPORTANT QUESTIONS FROM THE SMITHS

What questions should you ask when you are hiring a money manager?

The following questions are a very good starting point for learning if a particular manager is a suitable match for you:

1. *What is your investment strategy? (Is the strategy easily understood? Does it make sense to you?)*
2. *How long have you been managing assets using this strategy? (Has it been consistently used, or has the manager more recently adopted it? How much experience does the management team have?)*
3. *What is the performance—what are the returns and how much risk was taken? (Is the performance history documented? How has risk been quantified? How consistent are the returns—1 year, 3 year, 5 year, 10 year—versus a benchmark?)*
4. *What are the worst percentage drawdowns during the bad periods? (How much time did it take for the portfolio to get back to new highs?)*
5. *Will you communicate what we own and why? (Does the manager communicate when performance slides and things are not going well?)*

CONCLUSION AND RESOURCES

Summary Overview

With the help of our fictitious retirement couple, the Smiths, we have taken you through our secular outlook for stocks, bonds, and commodities. The Smiths spent their working years doing a wonderful job of saving by using a dollar cost averaging approach and essentially just "buying and holding" to build their wealth. The secular bull market in stocks and bonds that began in the early 1980s acted as a strong tailwind to compound wealth at far above-average levels for years on end. But, at the Smiths' retirement in 2000 two things changed. Instead of accumulating wealth, the Smiths entered the distribution phase of their retirement years and started drawing down their nest egg for living expenses. At the same time, the character of the stock market changed from secular bull to secular bear and a lost decade began. It may have taken 10 years to realize it, but the static buy-and-hold approach to investing was not working anymore. Years of stock market underperformance in addition to periodic distributions for day-to-day retirement living expenses weighed heavily on their carefully built nest egg.

The main theme we articulate in this book is that historically lost decades tend to occur back-to-back and form approximately 20-year secular bear periods. So, more of the same is on the way. Can the

Smiths continue with the same passive strategy and expect to meet their income needs for the rest of their lives? Or is there another more flexible alternative that can give them a fighting chance to survive financially?

Using history as a guide, this book details the reasons we expect *another* lost decade for stocks. Not only that, but we also alert readers to a possible secular change in the bond market from lower to higher yields. Bond investors have not had to deal with an adverse environment for more than 30 years. How many are prepared for this kind of change? Imagine the challenges maintaining wealth with both stocks and bonds in a secular bear market. And as the decade unfolds, if inflation becomes a major issue as we suspect it will, retirees and their portfolios will face an additional hurdle to overcome.

We believe the solution is for investors to pay careful attention to the repetitive nature of the business cycle for guidance. The secular bear climate warns there will be more frequent boom-and-bust periods. So the key to survival and prosperity is to apply a dynamic asset allocation approach. The proven sequential response of financial markets to business cycle swings is an invaluable tool that can help guide conservative portfolios through the market's inevitable ups and downs. The beauty for investors is that this approach provides the ability to anticipate change and act accordingly, as there are times when it is better to protect wealth and other times when it is more appropriate to grow wealth. This methodology is not an investment style or fad likely to someday go out of favor since business cycle activity repeats consistently as it has for over 150 years. There is a rhythm to the economy and markets that deserves investor attention. Better returns with less risk are the reward for those who learn and adopt this approach.

Investors face a daunting challenge as the secular bear stock market moves into its second decade. Our goal has been to assist investors in seeing the big picture and in gaining perspective on how to invest successfully during a secular bear market. The stock market still has a long journey ahead that will end with equities being undervalued, underowned, and underbelieved. This is simply how a secular bear market ends. We want you to arrive at the endgame with your wealth intact and ready to compound wealth easily in the next secular bull market.

You do not have to be a secular bear market victim. Change your mindset and incorporate a great game of defense into your investment game plan, rather than simply expecting easy profits that come with secular bull markets. Being more aware and paying attention to the stages of each business cycle will pay big dividends. Buy and hold or "buy and pray" are losing strategies in this secular bear market. Active asset allocation and careful sector investing changes will make for more profitable results with less volatility.

It is our sincere desire that we have helped readers better appreciate the economic and financial markets' secular themes in order to protect and grow their hard-earned wealth. Remember, Wall Street is designed to separate you from your money, while the ideas presented in this book are designed to separate you from Wall Street.

To the Smiths and all our readers, we wish good luck and good investing.

Additional Resources

The overriding purpose of this book is to help you to better understand the investment climate that will be with us in the next decade. With this knowledge and many of the tools we describe, we know that you will be well prepared to face the challenge. For further review, please remember to explore the material on the website at www.mhprofessional.com/mediacenter, which includes videos explaining our secular and business cycle outlooks and access to our charts in color. The coauthors and Pring Turner Capital Group will continue to provide research updates and publish helpful material to guide you along the way. We welcome you to follow along with free access to our latest research at www.pringturner.com and our blog at http://pringturner.com/blog/ that will update our outlook periodically.

This book was intended to be a concise yet detailed read on the secular outlook for the markets with an introduction to portfolio management techniques concerning the business cycle. For more detailed information on the subject we suggest you read Martin Pring's prior books, *The All-Season Investor* and *The Investor's Guide to Active Asset Allocation*. For an extensive handbook covering the subject of technical analysis, please refer to his highly regarded *Technical Analysis Explained*.

APPENDIX A

ADDITIONAL SIGNS OF SECULAR TURNING POINTS FOR EQUITIES

In this appendix we build on the material from Chapter 3 and consider some additional concepts that can help you identify secular turning points in equity markets. In this way it will be possible to paint a broader picture of what these important juncture points should look like. After all, the greater the number of pieces of the puzzle that come our way, the greater the odds that we will be able to spot the end of our current secular bear. Let's start off with a couple of additional measurements of value, which, as we noted in Chapter 3, should really be thought of as gauges of sentiment.

The Inverted Dividend Yield

Dividends are the actual returns that investors get for holding stocks, so their yield, like their P/E, also reflects the level of optimism or pessimism felt by market participants. If the yield is low, it indicates confidence that prices are likely to move higher. Why? Because the ultimate total return from a stock is a combination of current return (i.e., the dividend yield) and capital appreciation. If expectations are for higher prices, it means that investors are willing to settle for a low yield. On the other hand, at market lows, when prices have been falling for an extended period, yields are typically very high. This is because investors, having seen prices collapse, expect more of the same and need to be compensated for their perceived elevated risk in the form of a higher dividend yield. After all, if investors thought that stocks were going to explode in price, they would require no current yield at all.

High yields at secular lows also arise because one common cause of weaker stock markets is higher interest rates as the Fed seeks to cool the economy from end-of-the-cycle inflationary pressures. In order to compete with higher-yielding bonds, therefore, equity yields also need to rise. Since yields move inversely to prices, the dividend yield series in Chart A-1 is plotted in that way.

CHART A-1 Deflated U.S. Stock Prices Versus the Inverted S&P Composite Dividend Yield
This chart shows how dividend yields fluctuate from a buying zone low at the lower horizontal line at 7 percent to a very optimistic 3 percent at the upper horizontal line.

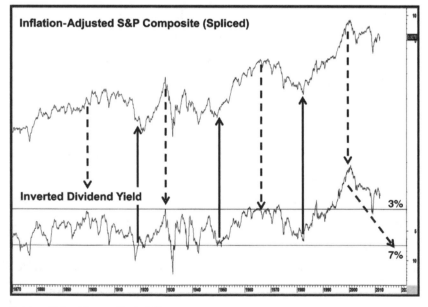

Source: Pring Turner Capital Group

ADDITIONAL SIGNS OF SECULAR TURNING POINTS FOR EQUITIES

The secular swings are not as obvious as those of the P/E in Chapter 3, but the turning points are all associated with extremes in valuation. When investors are optimistic, they are willing to settle for a paltry 2 to 3 percent yield. But when it comes to a secular low, they require a much more generous payout in the 6 to 7 percent range. The reading at the start of 2012 was just slightly more than 2 percent, clearly a long way from the average at secular lows of 6 to 7 percent.

While a high reading was attained at every secular low, it was not necessarily a sufficient condition. For example, in the mid–1870s the inverted yield moved to a very overextended reading only to see a bounce and a drop back to an even more extreme one. We see a similar setup in the 1900s and 1930s.

However, we can say that every secular bull market has been unable to get underway until a swing in the yield has taken it from a very overextended bull market reading to the 6 to 7 percent level. Thus, if the 2000–20?? secular bear ended in March 2009, it would have terminated at a dividend yield reading that was more akin to a secular top than a secular bottom. More likely, another decade of subpar stock market returns and rising dividend payouts could take us closer to the ultimate valuation level required for an end to the bear and the beginning of a new secular bull market.

Tobin's Q Ratio

Another method of measuring value was created by Yale economics professor and Nobel laureate James Tobin—hence the name Tobin's Q ratio. The Q ratio is the total market value of the stock market divided by the replacement cost of all the underlying companies. A value greater than one indicates that stock prices sell above their replacement cost and are therefore expensive, while a reading below one tells us that the market can theoretically be bought for less than replacement cost. If an individual corporation sells for less than one,

CHART A-2 Tobin's Q Ratio, 1900–2011

The Q ratio measures the replacement value of all listed stocks and is normally well above that level at secular peaks and at a 30 to 40 percent discount at secular lows.

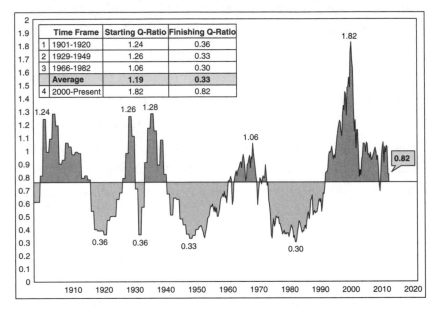

	Time Frame	Starting Q-Ratio	Finishing Q-Ratio
1	1901-1920	1.24	0.36
2	1929-1949	1.26	0.33
3	1966-1982	1.06	0.30
	Average	**1.19**	**0.33**
4	2000-Present	1.82	0.82

Source: The Manual of Ideas; Federal Reserve Statistical Release December 8, 2011: Z.1 Flow of Funds Accounts of the United States

this means that it is cheaper to buy it than build it. Chart A-2 offers a good understanding of value, information about current risk levels, and a method to assess probable returns for the long term.

Secular bear markets generally bottom when the ratio declines to a bargain level of less than 0.4, or when stock prices sell for just 40 percent of replacement value. The reading at the end of 2011, at 0.82, was considerably higher than that seen at the average secular low of 0.32.

The Response of Equities to Changes in the Money Supply

A final view of the secular trend comes with a comparison of real stock prices with the ratio between the S&P and money supply (M2) as shown in Chart A-3. This arrangement probably sets the scene better

CHART A-3 **CPI-Adjusted Stocks and the Equity/Money Supply Ratio**
Shaded areas represent secular bear markets. Arrows show cyclical reversals from
oversold levels in secular bear markets.

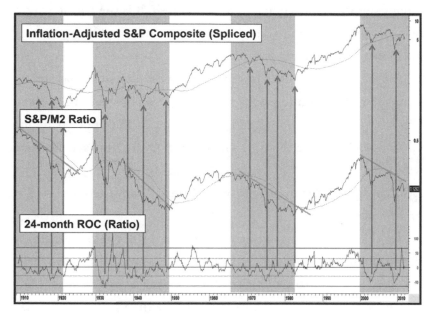

Source: Pring Turner Capital Group

than any in that it offers the perspective of the secular trend overlaid
on the cyclical trend. The concept behind this relationship is that an
increase in the money supply at some point feeds back into improved
economic activity and vice versa.

Until the market, in the form of the S&P 500, senses that this additional liquidity is actually going to have a positive effect, the ratio
declines. When the ratio finally responds to this injection of liquidity by rising, it signals the birth of a new cyclical or, at the end of a
very long-term decline, secular bull market. A declining ratio means
that the market is sensing that insufficient liquidity is being pumped
into the system in order to maintain a positive economy. In reality
the lead between the time when monetary expansion begins and the
economy responds is a varied one. This observation also applies to

the M2/stock relationship. That's why we look to changes in the direction of the ratio's trend to tell us when the market senses that the new money supply trend is going to have an effect. It is the reason why it often reverses direction relatively closely to major turning points in inflation-adjusted equity prices.

Note that the post–1929 low in the ratio developed in 1949, many years after the absolute price low that was established in 1932 (see Chart 2-1), or even the CPI-adjusted series in the upper panel of Chart A-3. The same thing happened during the next secular bear where the actual bottom in absolute prices formed in 1974, but the ratio continued declining into 1982. The CPI-adjusted series also bottomed in 1982.

The shaded areas flag secular bear markets since 1910. In the past their termination has been signaled in a timely and reliable fashion from a combination of the ratio crossing above its 96-month moving average (MA) and a violation of the then prevailing secular down trendline. The MA is represented by the dashed line. In this case the 96 months represent eight years or just over two business cycles worth of data. When it has been possible to construct a meaningful trendline and this has also been violated, another reasonably timely signal of an emerging secular bull is given. Of course this is not precise timing, but, after all, we are trying to identify a secular trend reversal that will probably last 18 to 20 years, so a few years here or there is not that material.

Since the year 2000 it has been possible to construct a fourth down trendline, which was actually intersecting with the 96-month MA at the start of 2012. This convergence of resistance points offers a very significant benchmark from which the next secular reversal can be identified. Two other useful benchmarks that will help to isolate a long-term reversal are the secular down trendline for the deflated S&P and its 180-month or 15-year MA.

From a primary trend aspect, the arrows show that most business-cycle associated bottoms during secular bear markets have developed when the rate of change of the S&P/M2 has reversed from a position close to or below the dashed oversold line. At the start of 2012 this momentum series clearly had some way to go before it would provide a positive signal. In this respect, it's important to note that while the vast majority of cyclical bulls that develop under the context of a secular bear are signaled in this way, there are some that are not.

While it is important to note the huge increase in liquidity that took place in the opening part of the decade, we also need to be aware of how that liquidity is being used. If, for example, money supply expands but people park this new money in a bank account or under the bed, it has no stimulatory effect. On the other hand, if they start to use it and production does not rise in proportion, prices will. That's the idea behind Chart A-4, which features on 18-month ROC of the velocity of M2. As you can see, this series lines up very well with the peaks and troughs in the CRB Spot Raw Industrials. The dashed arrows show when this normally consistent relationship has failed. If the increase in money supply is offset by a decline in its velocity (defined as GDP/M2), the oscillator will fall, and vice versa. As of the close of 2012, the oscillator is very overstretched on the downside but still falling. As long as this trend continues there are no inflationary consequences. However, when it starts to pick up again, implying that M2 velocity has picked up, that will be the time to expect a resumption of the secular uptrend in commodity prices, provided it has not been negated in the meantime.

The Role of Unstable Commodity Price Trends

In Chapter 3 we established that the nature of the long-term trend of commodity prices has an enormous effect on the direction of

CHART A-4 CRB Spot Raw Industrials Versus Velocity of Money

This chart shows the connection between business cycle–associated changes in commodity prices with the momentum of M2. Its low reading in February 2012 hints at a reversal sometime later that year or early 2013.

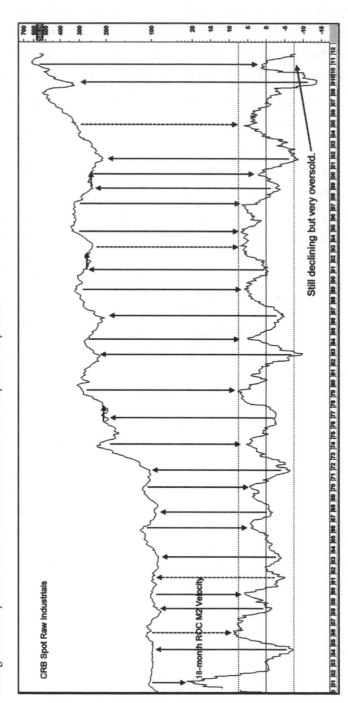

Source: Pring Turner Capital Group

the secular trend of CPI-adjusted stock prices. We concluded that gently rising, flat, or falling prices offered a benign environment in which stocks could flourish. However, when they become unstable in either direction for an extended period, this is a formula for a long-term decline in inflation-adjusted prices. Alternatively, it could result in a trading range for equities in absolute price terms.

We stated in earlier chapters that we expect the commodity secular bull market dating from 2001 to extend, principally because of its below-average duration at the end of 2011. By way of further justification for an inflationary view, the default policy of central banks is to resort to monetary expansion at the slightest sign of trouble. This means that commodity price volatility is usually experienced on the upside. However, there have been instances when downside instability in commodity prices has been responsible for specific phases of secular bear markets.

So what if we are wrong in our secular commodity uptrend assumption? What if the debt overhang has the effect that it normally does of cramping growth and offsetting the monetary printing presses with a consequential deflationary outcome, à la 1929 and 1932? How would we know? Well that's where the next two charts come in.

Chart A-5 compares real stock prices to a momentum measurement for commodity prices and further supports the idea that rapidly moving commodity prices in *either* direction are bearish for stocks.

The indicator itself expresses how each monthly level in the commodity index deviates from its 18-month MA, so it is more of a business cycle–associated barometer for equity prices than a secular one. A high reading indicates when the index is substantially above its 18-month MA and vice versa. This relationship demonstrates that *sharp commodity momentum rallies that develop from an extremely oversold condition are actually bullish for equities,* because they signify a recovery coming out of a deep recession. Other than

CHART A-5 Real Stock Prices Versus Commodity Momentum
Unusual commodity volatility on both the upside and downside usually results
in sharply lower equity prices. The arrows indicate that oversold reversals in the
commodity oscillator offer great buying opportunities for stocks.

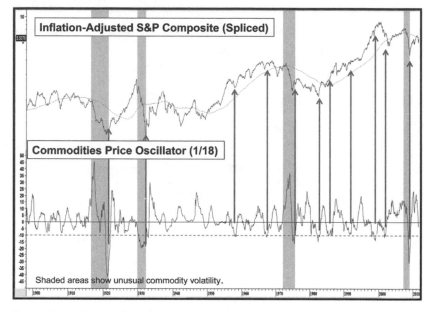

Source: Pring Turner Capital Group

that, unusually large swings in commodity prices adversely affect
equities. The shaded areas point up the greatest fluctuations, which
have also been associated with the worst equity bear markets in the
last 100 years or so. The arrows indicate when the oscillator comes
close to or briefly touches the −10 percent level and reverses to the
upside. You can see that these events are usually associated with
a bear market low or a quick but nasty shakeout such as the one
that developed in 1998. If you never appreciated the fact that equity
prices generally abhor instability, this chart brings you up to speed!

Quantifying Dangerous Commodity Instability

We have already established the broad connection between real stock
price declines and unstable commodity prices. However, the missing

ingredient is a more precise approach that we could use to identify positive and negative equity environments during the course of the business cycle.

Chart A-6, for instance, takes a slightly different tack because it actually measures environments of cyclical equity risk for inflation-adjusted equities and flags them with the light highlights. These periods were determined by our commodity instability model, which is described below. This is useful as a tactical device for allocating assets over the course of the business cycle. In addition it *quantifies* the type of commodity instability being experienced and therefore aids us in our quest to better appreciate whether the environment is approaching a destabilizing commodity rally or a disrupting decline.

CHART A-6 Real Stock Prices Versus the Stock/Commodity Model
This model effectively identifies cyclical bear markets for stocks, which are more pronounced in secular bear periods.

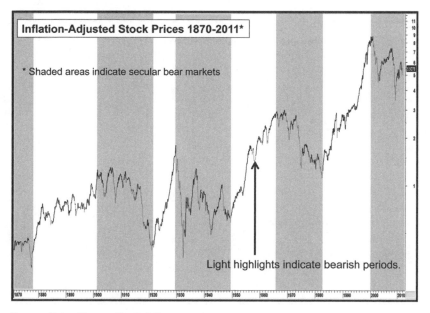

Source: Pring Turner Capital Group

The model takes three factors into consideration and also defines them. They are:

1. Dangerous periods of upside commodity volatility
2. Treacherous environments of declining commodity prices
3. A form of trend measurement that confirms whether equities are responding in a negative way to the defined environment

When either volatility condition is confirmed by the trend measure or the trend measure on its own is negative, it is assumed that equities are risky and should be avoided. By the same token if the trend is positive and neither volatility condition is in force, this is the all-clear sign to invest in equities.

The ingredients for the actual model are featured in Charts A-7 and A-8. Chart A-7 covers the bulk of the period since 1870, and Chart A-8 embraces more recent price action. Light highlights again indicate when bearish periods are identified in the model.

CHART A-7 Real Stock Prices Versus the Stock/Commodity Model, 1870–1982

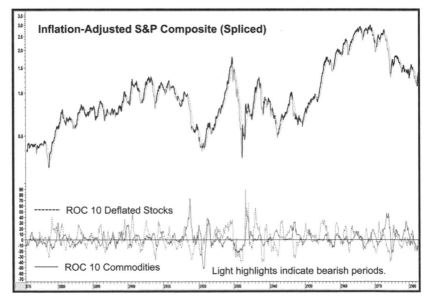

Source: Pring Turner Capital Group

In Chart A-7, the negative signals for inflation-adjusted stocks develop when two of three conditions are in force. First when the 9-month ROC (rate of change) for deflated equities and commodities are both below zero. In this case negative commodity momentum indicates a weak economy, and the bearish negative equity velocity confirms that stock prices are responding to it. It's also a way of showing that downside commodity instability is sufficient to have an adverse effect on stocks. If it weren't, then stocks would not be experiencing negative momentum.

Our second condition (Chart A-8) attempts to monitor situations when upside commodity momentum is excessive and therefore likely to harm stocks. For example, we know that a gentle rise in commodity prices is positive for equities because it reflects the fact that the economy is growing, but not in an overheated way. However, when

CHART A-8 Real Stock Prices Versus the Stock/Commodity Model, 1982–2011

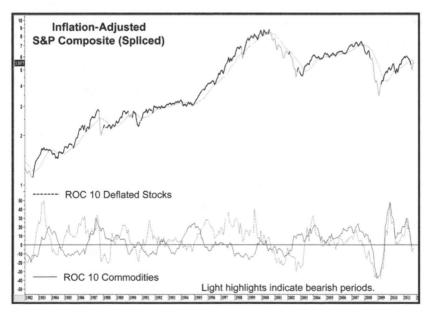

Source: Pring Turner Capital Group

193

commodity prices accelerate to the upside and stocks fail to respond, it is a signal that equities have started to factor in these inflationary pressures in a negative way. Stocks are a forward-looking indicator, so their reluctance to follow commodity prices higher means that they are anticipating that these end-of-cycle pressures will soon end in an economic contraction.

Our model measures this condition by subtracting a specified rate of change for inflation-adjusted equities from that of commodities. When the differential exceeds a specified amount, the second unstable commodity condition is met. It remains in force until a reading below the triggering level materializes.

The final model ingredient is that the deflated stock series must confirm the condition being signaled by its other two components. In other words, if either of the conditions is bearish, then deflated equities must also be below their 9-month moving average.

We can use the model from two points of view. First, the shaded areas in Chart A-6 show the secular bear markets that have evolved since the mid-nineteenth century. The light highlights indicate when the model was bearish, and it is fairly obvious that the indicated setbacks, for the most part, were pretty severe. The good news is that the model caught most of these declines. Secular bulls also experience primary trend declines, but these are far more benign.

The model catches most of them, but because of their ephemeral nature, the model is usually a bit late in signaling the all clear. The moral of the story is that if a secular bull is in force, investors are quickly bailed out, so the model does not deserve as much respect when on a sell signal. On the other hand, in a secular bear, sell signals indicate a much more risky environment, so those who ignore it do so at their peril.

This approach can also be used to help form a cyclical allocation strategy. By and large, an overweight position in equities would be appropriate when the model is bullish, whereas a trimmed down position would make more sense when it is negative.

The upper portion of Chart A-9 shows the equity line for the system using a fully invested position when the model is bullish (dark highlight) and there is no exposure during bearish periods (light highlight).

An original investment of $1,000 would have returned over $250,000 over the 130 years of the model. This assumes the receipt of a paltry 3 percent interest rate when out of the market (the average was 4.4 percent), but makes no allowance for commissions or slippage for the 104 trades. A buy-and-hold approach during the same period returned a $125,000 gain with far greater risk exposure. When using the CPI-adjusted series, the profits were, of course, much less at $67,000. However, the comparisons against the $13,000 buy-and-hold

CHART A-9 S&P Composite Versus the Equity Line for the Stock/ Commodity Model

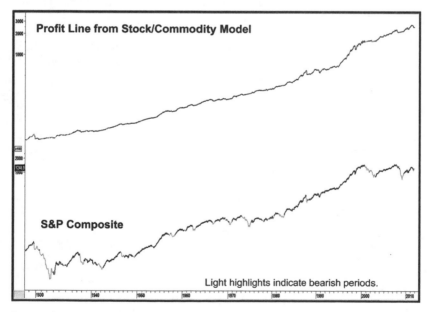

Source: Pring Turner Capital Group

approach were far superior—an approximate quintuple in the difference between the two results compared to a doubling for the absolute comparison. The reason was that during bear markets, when the system was largely in cash, the inflation-adjusted losses were much greater.

APPENDIX B

SUPPLEMENTARY OBSERVATIONS RELEVANT TO THE SECULAR COMMODITY BULL MARKET

In Chapter 4 we pointed out how inflation can slowly but surely eat away at portfolio values over the years and that the most likely outcome is for an extension of the secular bull market for industrial commodity prices for the balance of the current decade. In this section we examine two aspects of the inflation/deflation battle, the inflationary aspects of the recent unprecedented expansion in the monetary base and the deflationary consequences of the debt overhang and continued accumulation of obligations. First let's examine the issue of the rapid expansion in the monetary base.

Expansion of the Monetary Base—Is the Gas Already on the Fire?
The monetary base is the raw material for creating money. It comprises currency in circulation, member bank reserves held at the Fed, and vault cash. We all know that when the supply of money expands relative to the amount of goods in the system, price inflation results. The degree of the inflation will depend on changes in the velocity of circulation. When banks create loans, this has the effect of increasing the money supply. They are limited in their ability to do this by the fact that there is also a requirement for them to hold a certain proportion

of those loans in the form of reserves. These reserves also form part of the monetary base.

In September 2008 the Fed engineered a 180-degree turn as it reversed its policy from fighting inflation to one of promoting it. The objective was to stem the tide of deflation, and the vehicle was an expansion in the monetary base, which it controls by purchasing and selling assets on the open market. Purchasing assets held by the banks puts cash into the system, which is inflationary, and selling them drains it, which is deflationary. This was no ordinary change of heart because the scope of the operation was unprecedented. Economist Arthur Laffer in a June 11, 2009, *Wall Street Journal* article titled "Get Ready for Inflation and Higher Interest Rates," noted, "The percentage increase in the monetary base is the largest increase in the past 50 years by a factor of 10." He went on to point out that the bank reserve component of the base, which is where the system gets its leverage, had increased twentyfold. At that time the bank reserves comprised 50 percent of the base. This was significant since reserves—as opposed to currency in circulation, which is the other major base ingredient—are the foundation of loan creation and therefore money supply growth. Laffer went on to explain the consequences of these developments, "It's difficult to estimate the magnitude of the inflationary and interest-rate consequences of the Fed's actions because, frankly, we haven't ever seen anything like this in the U.S. To date what's happened is potentially far more inflationary than were the monetary policies of the 1970s, when the prime interest rate peaked at 21.5% and inflation peaked in the low double digits. Gold prices went from $35 per ounce to $850 per ounce, and the dollar collapsed on the foreign exchanges. It wasn't a pretty picture."

That was in 2009, and as you can see in Chart B-1 the base, after consolidating, resumed its upward path.

CHART B-1 Monetary Base, 1987–2011

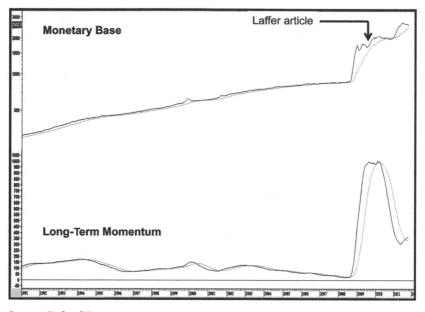

Source: Federal Reserve

Thus we have the gasoline and we have the fire, but we do not yet have the match to set it alight because banks at the beginning of 2012 had not expanded their loan portfolios to any great degree. If they had, it would be imperative for the Fed to reduce the base, either by selling Treasuries on the open market or by raising the reserve requirements on banks. (Banks are required to keep a certain amount of their assets in the form of reserves against the loans they create. Raising the requirement gives them less leeway to make loans.)

Selling Treasuries would put a significant amount of supply on the market and push up interest rates. Raising reserve requirements would put a lid on bank lending, and that too would have the effect of elevating rates. We are assuming here that the demand for credit would not immediately abate. Historically the Fed has been reluctant to raise rates as quickly as it should. After all, who wants to risk a recession, because a recession would take place if the Fed was to be too aggressive as was the case in 2000–2001 when it actually reined in the base.

Given the lopsided U.S. government debt structure, it could well be that such a policy would run the risk of tipping the inflation/deflation balance toward excessive deflation. This would undoubtedly extend the equity secular bear. We think it's important to remember that deflation can result in a sudden loss of confidence and the by-product of that is a sharp decline in equities. Just ask traders in the late 1870s and early 1930s about this. It was no coincidence that the unexpected 2008 stock market rout was caused by deflationary forces. By way of a footnote, an expansion in the monetary base has not been limited to the United States as it also expanded in Europe, Japan, China, and the United Kingdom in the 2002–2011 period. This is shown in Chart B-2,

CHART B-2 Total Assets of Major Central Banks, 2000–2011
The U.S. Federal Reserve has received considerable criticism concerning its excessive creation of liquidity. This chart shows that it's been a "team" effort as the European Central Bank, Bank of Japan, People's Bank of China, and the Bank of England have all joined in.

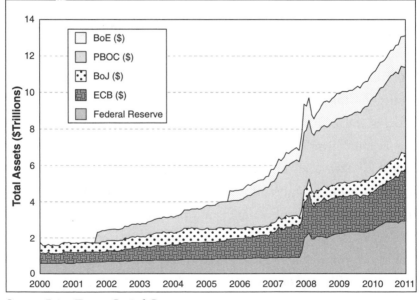

Source: Pring Turner Capital Group

where it can be seen that the expansion in central bank balance sheets has been a global "team" effort.

Chart B-3 examines the idea that commodity prices are influenced not just by changes in the money supply but also by those changes when adjusted by monetary velocity. In other words, while it is important to note the huge increase in liquidity that took place in the opening decade of the century, we also need to be aware of how it is being used. If, for example, the money supply expands but people park a lot of it in a bank account or under the bed, this results in far less stimulation than if it were used to purchase goods and services. As long as that is the case, increases in the money supply are benign, just like a can of gas placed near an unlit fire. On the other hand, if people start

CHART B-3 CRB Spot Raw Industrials Versus the Momentum of Money Supply Adjusted by Velocity
The lower panel contains an 18-month rate of change (ROC) of M2 adjusted for fluctuations in the velocity of circulation. The shaded areas flag when the oscillator is in a declining trend and when commodity prices usually decline. The 2004–2005 period was an exception to this rule.

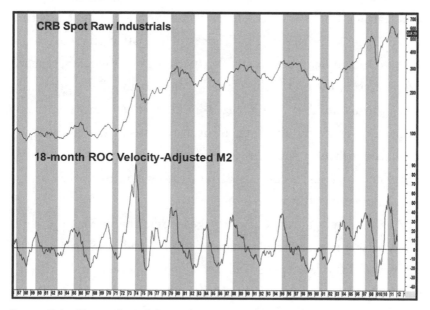

Source: Pring Turner Capital Group

to use that money so it circulates around at a fast pace, its influence on levels of economic activity and later on prices is much more powerful. It's the same effect as scattering the can of gas over logs and using a match to set it alight. In a crude way, the oscillator in the bottom panel of the chart attempts to gauge the relationship between changes in the money supply and its velocity (GDP/M2). The shaded areas roughly correspond to the declines in this momentum series, and you can see these periods line up very well with commodity bear markets, though the 2004–2005 experience shows this is not a perfect match. Neither would we expect it to be since commodity prices are determined by global forces, not just U.S. ones.

The Debt Overhang—Will It Result in Inflation or Deflation?

One significant factor hanging over the United States is excessive levels of public debt, which also has a bearing on whether the secular bear market in equities is likely to extend. In their book *This Time Is Different* (Princeton University Press, 2011), Kenneth Rogoff and Carmen Reinhart researched a data set of public debt covering 44 countries for up to 200 years. They concluded that a debt overhang becomes a problem for economic growth when public debt reaches 90 percent of the GDP. The United States, in 2009, was perilously close to this number (see Chart B-4). The 90 percent level is not a make-or-break number but an approximate one. For example, off-balance-sheet guarantees and creative accounting often make it difficult to assess a country's true debt level until a crisis brings everything out in the open.

As an example, the debt of mortgage lenders Fannie Mae and Freddie Mac was never officially guaranteed until the 2008 crisis. In the early part of the twenty-first century, any discussion of public liabilities in developed countries should also take into account the demographic challenges from a progressively aging population relative to

CHART B-4 U.S. Debt as a Percentage of the GDP, 1790–2009

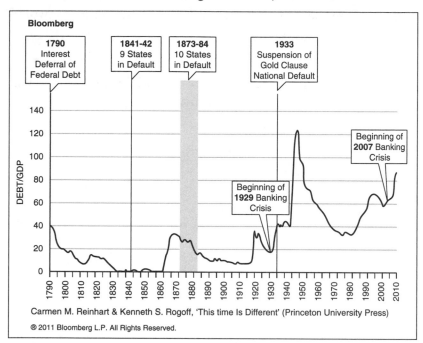

Source: Bloomberg L.P. All rights reserved.

workers. Their 90 percent threshold was largely based on periods prior to the escalation of pensions and healthcare, which suggests that these factors will act as an additional inhibitor of growth.

There are really only three ways to get out of a debt problem: inflate, default, or pay the debt down to a more comfortable level. A fourth possibility, growing out of the problem, becomes progressively more problematic the higher the ratio. All three of the other solutions are long-term negatives for equities. First, the amount of inflation required to do the job would have to be substantial. We have already seen how excessive inflation can be bearish for equities. Second, default would result in a loss of confidence, probably setting off a downward deflationary spiral. This would also likely extend the secular bear and lower price/earnings ratios. So too would the third alternative, paying off the debt and cutting expenditures. That would be the preferred solution, but the short-term economic pain it would cause would also result in an extension to the secular bear. The good news is that such a policy could ultimately restore confidence thereby possibly truncating its length by a few years. Political haggling will likely answer this issue in the next few months and set the course for the length of the second lost decade.

APPENDIX C

GLOBAL ASPECTS TO THE SECULAR BEAR MARKET IN STOCKS

O ur attention so far has been focused on the secular equity bear market in the United States, but this same phenomenon can be identified in other countries—mostly the developed ones.

What Is the Direction of the Global Secular Trend?
Since the early 1990s, the overall trend of the correlation between individual countries, as we might expect, is one of a closer-knit global financial community as markets around the world are gradually becoming more and more correlated. This arises not only because of institutional changes, such as the advent of 24-hour trading, increased international listings, international ETFs (which permit instant trading in international markets), and so on. Also important is the fact that companies are diversifying their operations globally. This means that, although they may be associated with the country in which they are domiciled, the bulk of their earnings comes from outside that domicile. Since the world is becoming more and more integrated, it is worth addressing whether the U.S. secular bear stands alone or is replicated in other countries.

The first place to start would be a CPI-adjusted measure for global equities. This is shown in Chart C-1 for the Morgan Stanley Capital

CHART C-1 MSCI World ETF (CPI-Adjusted) Versus the S&P Composite (CPI-Adjusted), 1967–2012
This chart shows that global markets like the United States have been in a secular market since the start of the century.

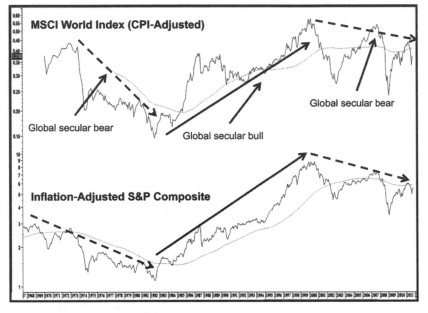

Source: Pring Turner Capital Group

International (MSCI) World Stock ETF, which has been spliced to its tracking index. This series has also been deflated by a global CPI, as published by the OECD (Organisation for Economic Co-operation and Development). As you can see, global equities come into the chart in a secular downtrend and remain there until 1982. A subsequent rally takes the index to a secular high in 2000 after which it begins a secular bear market. We conclude that it is a secular bear because the primary trend peaks and troughs since 2000 have been moving in a sequentially lower pattern. As you can see, there is a fairly close tie-in with U.S. experience between the global and U.S. series. We have to be a bit careful though, because in the early years the U.S. market represented a huge weighting in the world series. To some extent it could be argued that we were comparing oranges to oranges.

CHART C-2 **MSCI World ETF (CPI-Adjusted) Versus the German DAX (CPI-Adjusted), 1969–2012**
Germany and the World Index are closely correlated.

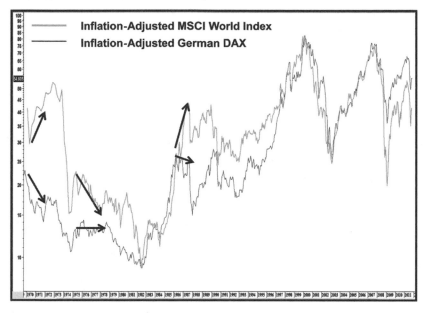

Source: Pring Turner Capital Group

The U.S. weighting is still significant but has definitely shrunk as emerging countries have come to the fore.

Chart C-2 compares the performance of the CPI-adjusted global series to the German DAX deflated by the German CPI. The experience is very similar, though in earlier years the trajectories did differ for a while as flagged by the arrows. Since the current secular bear began in 2000, the trajectories have been much closer thus indicating the stronger link between markets around the globe. Needless to say, our analysis of real German equities leads us to a draw a secularly bearish conclusion.

Japan: A Leading Indicator in Secular Bears

In the current cycle, the leading indicator of secular bear markets is Japan. Chart C-3 indicates that it has met the average U.S. magnitude

CHART C-3 Nikkei (CPI-Adjusted) and Price Swings in Excess of 25 Percent, 1975–2012

This chart shows the devastation wreaked on Japanese equities since 1989.

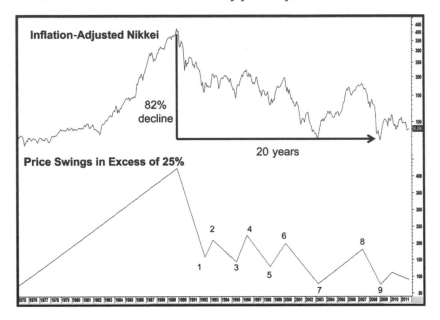

Source: Pring Turner Capital Group

(82 percent inflation-adjusted) and duration (approximately 20 years) standards.

You can also see that if 25 percent price swings are considered, the market has experienced nine waves which is far more than any U.S. secular bear experience. Indeed, by way of showing how poor the Japanese performance has been, current CPI-adjusted prices for the Nikkei at the end of 2011 were not far above 1963 levels.

Chart C-4 compares this CPI-adjusted Nikkei with that of the S&P. In this case the S&P data have been lagged by 126 months so that the two secular peaks coincide. The date scale on the X axis is for Japan. The waves in the lower panel compare the progress of these two series in a more simplistic way. Obviously they are not identical, but what is striking is that the two trading patterns are so close, thereby demonstrating

CHART C-4 **Real Japanese Versus Real U.S. Stock Prices, 1984–2011**

In a broad way, inflation-adjusted U.S. equity prices are following their Japanese counterparts.

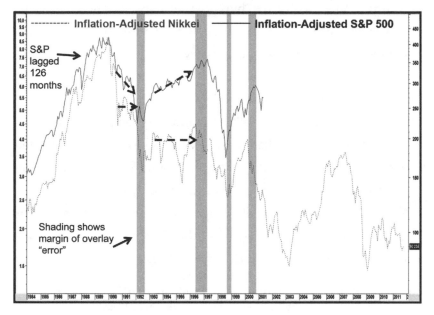

Source: Pring Turner Capital Group

that trends in mass psychology are similar both in terms of time and geography. When first viewed, the overlay for the U.S. 2000–2011 experience looks to be very similar to that of Japan. However, while the turning points are fairly near in terms of time, the price action in between can differ considerably. Some of this action has been flagged with the dashed arrows. The shaded areas are there to remind us that while the turning points of the major waves are reasonably close, they have differed by as much as 11 months. In effect, while interesting, this overlay chart should in no way be used for forecasting the future course of U.S. equities but more as a guideline to demonstrate the common underlying psychology applicable to secular bear trends. Down the road the U.S. market may experience some of the characteristics previously seen at secular turning points. If it does, it may also be possible to confirm that a reversal in Japanese fortunes had already taken place. In that way Japanese price action could be used as supplementary evidence for a U.S. turn. Consequently, we think that Japanese progress should be closely monitored in the future for it could well prove to be a very early leader for the next U.S. secular bull market.

Other Countries and the Global Secular Bear

Many may be wondering about China and the great promise it holds. After all, this market peaked in 2007 several years after the United States. In that respect, Chart C-5 shows that the Shanghai Index experienced a bubble of its own. This is evidenced by the extremely high reading in the 18-month rate of change in the lower panel. To put this elevated level into perspective, two other bubble peak readings are also shown. These are the historic 1980 gold peak and the Nasdaq peak

CHART C-5 Shanghai Composite and an 18-Month ROC, 1994–2012
This chart demonstrates that the Chinese equity market in 2007 had reached a higher level of euphoria than gold in 1980 or the Nasdaq in 2000.

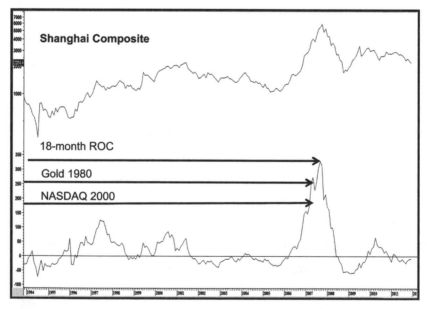

Source: Pring Turner Capital Group

in 2000. As you can see, the 2007 reading for the Shanghai composite reached a higher level than either of them. Momentum, it should be understood, is a way of statistically reflecting swings in sentiment in any market. We know from the experience of looking at other time periods and markets that a reading in the 18-month ROC in excess of 200 percent is very unusual. The reason is that it takes an immense amount of bullish sentiment to double the price of any security in such a relatively short time span. Usually, when people elevate prices that much and that quickly, it means that they are getting way ahead of the emerging fundamentals. Consequently, decisions being made are careless, and a lengthy period of ranging action or actual price erosion is almost always required to bring the situation back into balance.

There have been exceptions to this rule, but they are few and far between. In this respect Table C-1 shows all the 18-month ROC readings in excess of 200 percent that we have observed in our extensive database. To put this in perspective, the highest 18-month reading ever seen was 124 percent for the S&P Composite in 1844. It barely rose above 100 percent at the 1929 peak! The final column in the table shows how long it has taken to surpass the market reading registered at the ROC high. This is a far from precise approach because of the varying nature of the price action. Those labeled N/A in the fourth column mean that at the start of 2012 the high referred to had never been surpassed. The blanks in the fifth column mean that too little time has elapsed to offer meaningful results since the ROC peaked very recently in 2010 or 2011. It's obviously far too early to appreciate the effects of these overstretched reversals. The bottom line from all this is the suggestion that the 15-year average period needed to reach a recovery high should be taken with a grain of salt. Nevertheless, the implication from a +200 percent reversal in an 18-month ROC raises the odds that prices will decline sharply and/or experience a major trading range extending for more than five years and probably much

TABLE C-1 Recovery Time Following an 18-Month ROC Reading Above 200 Percent

This table shows that when a market reverses from a gain in excess of 200 percent achieved in an 18-month period, it usually results in a secular peak.

Market	ROC Reading	Date of High	Date of recovery High	Time (years)
Palladium	332	Mar–80	Mar–98	18
Palladium	201	Jan–01	N/A	10
Palladium	232	Apr–98	Nov–99	1
Palladium	240	Dec–10	N/A	
Platinum	264	Feb–80	Nov–05	15
NASDAQ	274	Mar–00	N/A	11
Silver	212	May–74	Jul–78	4
Silver	542	Feb–80	Mar–11	31
Nikkei	217	Jan–53	Mar–56	3
BCI Commerciale	238	May–81	Apr–85	4
BCI Commerciale	272	May–86	Jun–97	11
Shanghai Composite	327	Sep–07	N/A	4
Bombay	205	Apr–92	Jul–99	7
Coffee	235	Apr–77	N/A	34
Coffee	271	Sep–94	Feb–97	3
Cocoa	237	May–77	N/A	34
Sugar	513	Nov–74	Aug–80	6
Sugar	449	Oct–80	N/A	31
Athens SE	618	Oct–87	Sep–89	2
Athens SE	478	Jul–90	Mar–98	8
ATX	218	Mar–90	4-Apr	14
Cotton	240	11-Feb	N/A	
FT Gold Mines	309	Apr–74	Sep–80	6
FT Gold Mines	295	Oct–80	N/A	31
Heating Oil	204	Aug–00	Jan–03	13
Helsinki General	228	Feb–94	Sep–96	2
Helsinki General	302	Mar–00	N/A	11
Copper	207	Apr–74	5-Apr	31
TSX Gold Shares	272	Sep–80	N/A	31
Wheat	327	Jan–74	Jun–07	33
Average	**299**			**15**

Source: Pring Turner Capital Group

longer. This is because it takes time and usually a lot of it to work off the excessive bullish psychology associated with the ROC peak. The point of the exercise then is to underscore the fact that the Chinese market in all probability began some kind of secular trading range or actual bear in CPI-adjusted terms in 2007.

Finally, we take a look at the Italian and Indian markets as adjusted by their respective CPIs as published by the OECD. They are shown in Chart C-6. Note that the Italian market peaked in real terms in 1966. Since then it has undergone a secular bear and bull and has, since 2000, experienced another secular bear. The 2011 violation of the light up trendline dating from 1980 does not argue well for its future.

The inflation-adjusted Indian market, on the other hand, remains in a long-term secular bull. If the 2009 low is taken out, that would

CHART C-6 Inflation-Adjusted Italian and Indian Markets, 1964–2012
This chart compares the secular experience of two countries with different population pyramids.

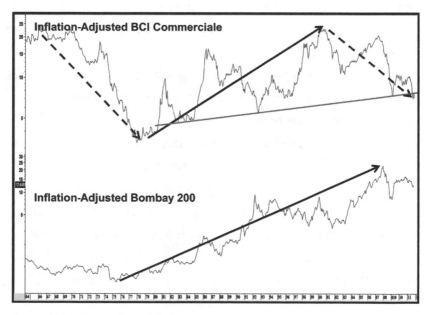

Source: Pring Turner Capital Group

213

set up a series of declining primary trend peaks and troughs and that would suggest to us that India had entered the global secular bear. Until then it is wiser to assume that the secular uptrend was still intact.

Two Structural Factors That Appear to Influence Secular Trends

By way of an aside, it would appear that the food for secular bears in individual countries comes from long-term structural imbalances in both debt structures and population pyramids. Figure C-1, for example, compares the population pyramids for Italy and India.

Ideally, a population pyramid set for growth has a very large base relative to its top. This means that a substantial part of the population is in a productive age bracket and that the smaller number at the top means relatively few dependents. Senior citizens as a group act as a drag since they are net consumers of resources.

If you recall, Italy has been in a severe secular bear, but India has so far escaped. Not surprisingly, India's population pyramid has a very wide base relative to its top. Compare that to Italy, where we see a trend toward top heaviness. Little wonder that Italy has been struggling.

A good population pyramid is not a guarantee that a country will avoid a secular bear market because other factors obviously come into play. Other things being equal, spotting a country with a favorable population pyramid offers a good starting point. In that respect Figure C-2 shows two countries with two potentially bullish long-term factors, a positive population pyramid and abundant resources. If we are correct in our assumption of a long-term bull market in commodity prices these two, Brazil and South Africa, should do very well.

Our second broad point concerning structural problems has to do with debt. An excess of dependent senior citizens is a kind of tax on growth, but just as important, it is an excess of debt. That's because the servicing of that debt robs society of valuable

FIGURE C-1 Population Pyramids for Italy and India
The lower the step, the younger the age. India has a favorable pyramid because a large number of young people are supporting a small number of senior citizens, a perfect setup for a long-term bull market. In Italy, we see the opposite structure.

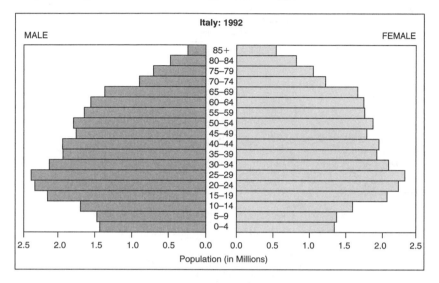

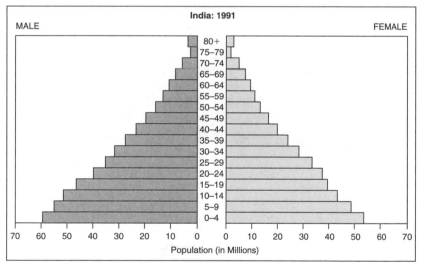

Source: U.S. Census Bureau, International Database

resources that could otherwise be used for investment. Countries with a population pyramid problem and overindebtedness are receiving a double hit. In that respect Table C-2 shows that two of

FIGURE C-2 Population Pyramids for Brazil and South Africa
Brazil and South Africa are well structured population-wise to develop economically.

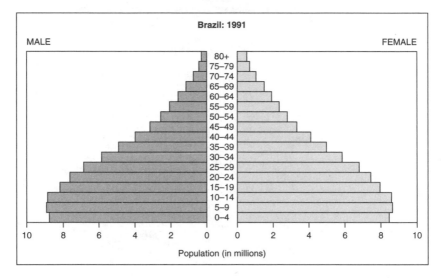

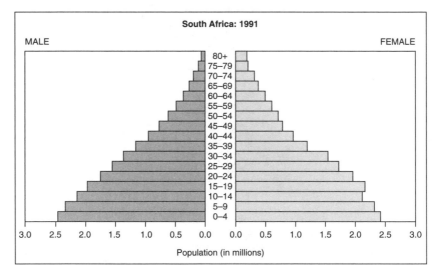

Source: U.S. Census Bureau, International Database

the worst-performing markets in recent decades, Japan and Italy, are at the top of the government net debt as a percentage of GDP.

By the same token other countries cited as potential secular bear escapees have a significantly lower debt-to-GDP ratio. Most notable

TABLE C-2 Country Debt as a Percent
of GDP

Japan	220%
Italy	119%
United States	94%
Brazil	67%
India	64%
South Africa	34%
Indonesia	27%

Source: International Monetary Fund, 2010

are South Africa (34 percent) and Indonesia (27 percent). We did not mention earlier that Indonesia also has a very favorable population pyramid. This seems to be an optimistic note on which to end this appendix.

APPENDIX D

A GUIDED TOUR OF ASSET ROTATION AROUND THE BUSINESS CYCLE

C hapter 8 described the six stages of the business cycle in broad terms. This appendix takes us a step deeper into what these individual phases of the cycle look like. From there we can discuss what kind of assets make the most sense at each stage.

A Roundup of the Six Individual Stages of the Business Cycle
Here is a more detailed look at the six stages of the business cycle beginning with stage 1.

Stage 1 (Only Bonds Are Bullish)
CASH
When we refer to cash, we are really talking about high-quality liquid assets, such as three-month commercial paper, three-month T-bills, and of course money market funds. Basically, we can think of any one of these assets as a good-quality debt instrument with a maturity of less than one year. Anything greater than that and we are exposing ourselves to the market risk of fluctuating interest rates. Bank CDs that cannot be redeemed prior to maturity without a large penalty are

not appropriate because we need to have some degree of flexibility to rebalance the portfolio when conditions change.

In stage 1 of the business cycle, it makes sense to hold a substantial amount of cash because two of our asset classes, namely stocks and commodities, are both in bear markets. The stock market and inflation hedge assets both correlate negatively with cash. It therefore has a stabilizing or capital preservation function.

Also, cash usually offers a high rate of return relative to the rest of the cycle because short-term interest rates are just coming off their cyclical peak. The amount of return will vary from cycle to cycle and will depend on the direction and maturity of the secular trend. For example, the approximate return on cash at the start of stage 1 in October 1981, at the top of the inflationary secular trend, was 14.7 percent. This compared to 6.6 percent in the opening month of stage 1 in June 2001, which was 20 years into the post–1981 secular deflationary trend. In early 2012 it was close to zero, but we think that these ridiculously low numbers are temporary.

BONDS

Stage 1 offers the best return for bonds during the whole cycle. Positive returns begin after prices have suffered through a bear market. From an asset allocation point of view, this is the optimal point in the cycle to be taking a very aggressive stance. If you refer back to Figure 7-1, you will see that this phase of the cycle develops during the downward part of the recession. At this time bondholders have everyone on their side. First, credit demands are falling like a stone because businesses are battening down the hatches and lowering those breakeven points as fast as they can. Second, the Fed is now committed to fighting the unemployment battle, so it is pumping money into the banking system as fast as it can. This falling demand and expanding supply of credit reduces interest rates. Since bond prices move inversely to interest rate, good-quality bonds have only one way to go, and that is up. Stage 1 is therefore a time when maturities can be extended since this will result in more upside leverage at a time when the risks are lowest. The actual maturities will depend on the risk tolerance of the individual investor. In a general sense, though, stage 1 is the time when the (tactical) bond allocation should be at the higher end of the risk tolerance level for that particular individual, which will depend on such factors as age, financial circumstances, stage of life, and personality.

Specific investment decisions will also depend on the point at which a stage 1 is identified. With the benefit of hindsight, it is always possible to identify the final bear market low in bond prices. However, in the real world it is usually necessary for some time to elapse before it is evident that a low has been reached. Let's say that you are using a positive 12-month moving average crossover to identify a change in trend. In this case it will normally take some time for the price to rally up and cross the average. By that time, prices may have advanced 25 to 30 percent. This means that the bull market will already have realized quite a bit of its potential, so your reward-risk ratio will not be as attractive as it would have been had you been able to identify stage 1 closer to the outset. Under such circumstances you would be advised to buy fewer bonds than you normally would at this stage of the cycle. Alternatively, you could buy just as many bonds but shorten their maturity thus reducing market risk. For example, expose yourself to the Lehman 7–10 year (IEF) ETF rather than the 20 year series (TLT).

Some stage changes are easier to spot than others because of the quality and quantity of the signals being triggered by the various indicators that we describe later. If you are able to spot a number of signals all pointing in the same direction, this will increase the odds that you have correctly identified that turning point. It will raise the probability that an above-average stage 1 bond move is under way.

On the other hand, if the indicators are wishy-washy or contradictory, such uncertainty calls for a less aggressive and more conservative posture. If you are wrong, you will not have lost money, merely a badly signaled opportunity, and there are plenty of those.

It's a good idea to try to qualify the signals, just like the star ratings for good restaurants. If you get what you consider to be a five-star signal and prices are not overextended, then by all means take on more risk. However, if it's a one- or two-star signal, then be more cautious. A five-star signal would consist of several indicators all pointing in a favorable direction for bonds and at a time when prices are trading close to their bear market lows. A one-star signal would develop with just one or two indicators barely in bullish territory with, perhaps, some contradiction from one or more other series.

Earlier we mentioned that stage 1 is a *good* time to purchase *good*-quality bonds. The word *good* has been emphasized because stage 1 can be a dangerous time to buy low-quality paper. Remember, this is the point in the cycle when economic activity is starting to pick up momentum on the downside. It is therefore a period, like stage 4 or, occasionally, early in stage 2 when the greatest danger of a credit default exists. Even if the company whose bonds you own remains solvent, there is almost surely going to be a spill-over effect if another company in a similar industry with an equivalent quality rating to your company's defaults. Be assured that the market will quickly factor in the growing risk in the only way it knows—lower prices.

If you own corporate bonds, it is also important to review the call features of those contained in your portfolio or for which you may be considering a purchase. Call features allow the issuing corporation to *call* or buy back the bonds at a stipulated price. If the bond has a particularly high coupon relative to current rates, there is an incentive to buy it back and reissue it at the then prevailing lower rate of interest. Under such circumstances you will be denied the ability to realize the full price appreciation potential from declining corporate yields. A simple solution is to buy a diversified corporate bond ETF such as the iBoxx $ Investment Grade Corporate Bond Fund (LQD).

EQUITIES

Stage 1 is generally a bad time for most stocks, but there are some sectors that are often able to buck the trend. Utilities, financials, some consumer staples, and, occasionally, transports often make money in stage 1. Home builders are another interest-sensitive group that do well in the early part of the cycle. These, of course, are average tendencies, which means that these sectors do not necessarily gain in every stage 1 of every cycle. A stage 1 signal, then, does not give you carte blanche to buy these sectors, since each cycle must be judged on its own merits.

INFLATION HEDGE

Since the economy is weak in stage 1, commodity prices and other inflation hedge assets are usually falling. This is often early on in the bear market because they still have stage 2 to endure. Inflation hedge assets are therefore avoided at this time. Equities in the materials sector, for the most part, have a terrible time in stage 1.

Stage 2 (Only Commodities Are Bearish)

CASH

Cash is less important in stage 2 because stocks have now bottomed, and this is typically the phase when the equity market experiences its broadest and fastest advance. The rewards are high, and the risks are at their lowest, so this is the stage when a substantial part of the portfolio should be allocated to stocks. Once again the degree of equity allocation will depend on personal circumstances. However, whatever they are, this should be the point when your equity allocation is greatest. Remember, the opportunity cost of holding lower-yielding cash is now quite high because it is very difficult to buy a losing stock market sector in stage 2.

BONDS

Experience shows that the returns for owning bonds remain attractive, though less so than during stage 1. This means that most portfolios should still contain some long-dated debt instruments. Remember, there is another bullish phase for bonds yet to come. However, since equities offer a higher *relative* return than bonds at this time, a rotation into stocks certainly makes sense. Also, since the stock market is signaling an economic recovery, the risk of default from holding high yield bonds has declined. It therefore makes sense to invest a small amount of capital into a well-diversified high yield bond mutual fund or ETF such as the iShares iBoxx $ High Yield Corporate Bond Fund (Symbol HYG). The gain from this move will be threefold: first a higher yield; second, higher prices resulting from a general bull market in bonds; and third, as confidence grows, the appreciation from "junk" bonds will be greater than governments or AAA corporates because of the contraction in the yield spread between them.

EQUITIES

The equity portion of the portfolio should now be quite substantial as money flows in from the redemption of cash together with some bond sales. The amount of bond liquidation will again be determined by individual circumstances. Those who require a substantial income will obviously retain more bonds than others who do not. Even so, it is often possible to pick up yield in the utility sector and some blue chips that are paying good dividends. The advantage of these high yielding stocks is that they offer a greater potential, not only for capital gains but also for income enhancement through possible dividend hikes.

The degree to which a portfolio should load up on stocks is also determined by the market environment at the time. What is the quality of the stage 2 signal? Have stocks already risen sharply from their lows by the time this is realized? And so forth. Usually the first or second cut in the discount rate is followed by very strong equity markets. However, if the market is already up by 25 percent from its lows, it will *already* have factored in some pretty good news. Consequently, it makes sense to wait for a pullback. This is often extremely difficult because rising markets attract bullish emotions and greater confidence. However, this is often a time when self-discipline pays off. Those who jump in, however, should be prepared to live through the inevitable correction and await those stage 3 and 4 gains.

Occasionally a change in industry group leadership takes place during the latter phase of stage 2. Some of the early leaders such as utilities and consumer staples (household items, tobacco, beverages, food products, etc.) begin to underperform the S&P composite. They continue to rise in absolute price but are overtaken in performance by consumer cyclicals, otherwise known as *consumer durables*. These would include big-ticket consumer items such as autos and major appliances.

INFLATION HEDGE

The economy may have lost its downside momentum in this stage, but it still continues to decline until the end of stage 2. This means that in most cycles, commodity prices continue to fall. Inflation hedge equities, such as resource-based stocks, often bottom coincidentally with the major averages, but apart from a good bounce, they generally underperform until the latter part of the cycle. Indeed, they occasionally rally off the bear market low and then undergo a close test of that bottom before taking off on a sustainable bull market. Gold usually leads major commodity price turns. Unfortunately the lead varies from cycle to cycle, sometimes coinciding and at other times leading by a year or more. This means that occasionally gold shares experience a bottom close to that of the market itself and often begin a bull market in both an absolute and relative sense. For example, they bottomed in June 1982, a couple of months ahead of the major averages, which experienced their lows in August. Gold shares are therefore a wild card in the deck and often move independently of any rational theories. The one thing we can say is that when the ratio of stocks to gold is declining, this is usually bearish for stocks. This is generally true from both a cyclical and secular aspect.

Stage 3 (Everything Is Bullish)

CASH

Stage 3 offers the lowest relative return of the cycle as all other asset classes are bullish. This is the point at which cash reserves should be held to a minimum since there are far better low-risk opportunities elsewhere.

BONDS

When stage 3 comes to an end, bond prices will be in a bear market. A progressive and gradual reduction of debt market exposure is therefore appropriate as this phase of the cycle unfolds. This can be achieved by paring back your bond position or reducing exposure to price risk from the eventual rise in yields. This is achieved by reducing the average maturity of the bond portfolio. Consequently, bonds continue to rise at the start of stage 3. However, as this phase develops, the opportunity cost of holding them increases as they eventually offer a negative return while stocks and inflation hedge offer positive ones. By the start of stage 4 zero-coupon bonds with a maturity greater than five years or coupon bonds in excess of seven years should be liquidated.

The big conflict is within the yield curve itself. An example of a normal yield curve is shown in Figure D-1. The normal shape for the yield curve involves a lower interest rate for shorter-term maturities and higher ones at the long end of the spectrum. The higher yield for longer maturities compensates investors for the greater market risk associated with longer periods. As stage 3 comes to a close, investors are faced with the need to protect their portfolios from the bond bear market, which is just getting under way. In order to do this, they will have to give up something in the form of current return since cash pays less at this point in the cycle. One compromise is to shorten the maturity, not to money market maturities, but to, say, three- to five-year bonds. By doing this, some capital depreciation will take place, but the loss of current return will not be as great as, say, moving from a 20-year maturity to a 3-month maturity. A lot depends on the yield

FIGURE D-1 **Hypothetical Yield Curve**

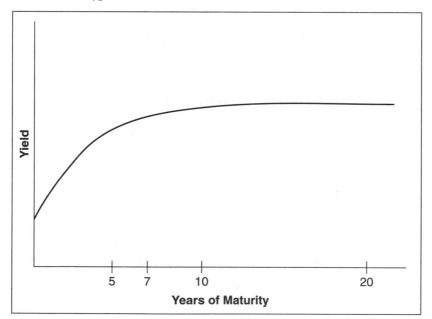

Source: Federal Reserve

differentials themselves as well as an assessment of how severe the oncoming inflationary pressures might be.

If you are confident that the prevailing trend is deflationary and that it has further to run, this could be a good strategy. However, if it appears that a secular inflationary trend has just begun, the risks of holding medium-term maturities would be quite high. In Figure D-1, you can see that the yield rises rapidly until around the seven-year point. After that, there is not much to be gained and a lot more to be risked. You would obtain more or less the same current yield at six or seven years as at twenty years, but the capital risk would be substantially less. Of course, if you can forgo more income, the safest place to be would be in the less than one-year area.

At smartmoney.com, it is possible to "play" with the yield curve using a Java applet that shows various yield-curve scenarios for different periods in the past. The site also explains yield-curve concepts such as normal, inverted, steep, and flat.

The final way in which the bond portfolio could be rotated would be to extend the process begun in the previous phase, which is to increase the allocation to high yield mutual funds. Such a move offers a higher rate of return. Also, because the economy is in the early stages of recovery, the risk from default is still quite low. Moreover, in many cycles we see prices of low-quality bonds peak after those of higher-rated paper because of confident yield-hungry investors.

STOCKS

Since commodity prices have now begun their bull market, commodity-related equities should be improving in relative performance. We may find that this comes at the expense of early cycle leaders such as interest-sensitive groups. In absolute price terms though, everything should be doing well. However, keep in mind that bull markets do not go straight up without interruption. They are subject to intermediate corrections which are designed to throw doubts on the validity of the primary trend. Also, specific industries that *should* be doing well in this stage may not be because of their own individual structural problems. A rotation, where early groups such as interest-sensitives actually decline, can take place toward the end of stage 3, but a price decline is more likely to start when interest rates begin their bull market in stage 4; often their bear markets are delayed until stage 5.

Stage 3 is also a time when it is possible to take on more risk, and this means that stocks with a lower beta may be added to the portfolio. This is not the same thing as saying that quality control should be abandoned and that you should take on additional risk regardless of the consequences. However, this is a phase when stocks are advancing on a broad front. Provided that the technical position is sound, this a time when the judicious addition of a couple of volatile stocks makes sense because it is possible in this environment to go after more reward with less fear of downside risk.

INFLATION HEDGE

Now that commodities have bottomed, it is appropriate to give greater emphasis to inflation-sensitive equities such as mines, oils, and basic industries. It is now possible to buy commodity-related no-load mutual funds, and, of course, commodity-related sector exchange-traded funds. However, at this point it is wise to increase the inflation hedge portion of your portfolio in order to participate in the commodity bull market that has just begun.

Stage 4 (Bonds Begin a Bear Market, but Stocks and Commodities Remain Bullish)

CASH

Rates tend to trace out a kind of saucer pattern at bottoms as they gradually work their way higher. This is not true of every bottom as the 1958 experience will attest, but a gradual rise in rates is more typical of a slow but deliberate improvement in the economy. Cash allocation at this time of rising rates, strong equities, and inflation hedge performance should be kept to a minimum.

BONDS

If you haven't already started reducing your level of bond exposure, now is your last chance before serious asset price erosion is likely to set in. The retention of high yield bond mutual funds or ETFs is one way of protecting current income for a little longer since these issues tend to top out in price after higher-quality instruments peak. Also, the risk of credit default, in a general sense, is still low, so the spread between low- and high-quality paper shrinks for a while longer— until stage 5.

STOCKS

Now is the time to step up the process of rotating from early cycle leaders, such as utilities, financials, telecommunications, and transports, into earnings-driven groups. These would include resource-based and basic industry. Midcycle leaders, such as technology, healthcare, consumer discretionary durables, and industrials are also strong relative performers at this time and should therefore be given a healthy allocation. Sometime during stage 4, if not just before, the early cycle leaders that protected us in stage 1 start a new cycle of underperformance, if not an actual price decline in absolute terms. Please remember that these comments are generalizations and do not necessarily apply to every group in every cycle. Sometimes financials, normally an early market leader, will linger until stage 5 before commencing their bear market. A lot depends on investors' attitudes to the emerging fundamentals. Usually they respond to them in the expected way, but there is a delayed effect. However, if you stick consistently to the rough trends outlined here, the odds favor superior long-term invest-ment performance.

INFLATION HEDGE

Stage 4 remains positive for commodities and commodity-related equities. Therefore, these should therefore continue to represent a significant portion of your allocation. What is *significant* will depend on the allocation strategy of each individual. Since this is a volatile sector, conservative investors with capital preservation and income generation on their minds are advised to make a relatively small allo-cation, more as a small inflation hedge than a way of making a lot of money quickly.

Stage 5 (Only Commodities Are Bullish)

CASH

Now that risk in the stock market has increased and money market yields have grown, it is appropriate to make a more substantial alloca-tion to cash.

BONDS

Inflationary pressures in the financial markets now become more obvious, so owning bonds is a very high-risk business. This is espe-cially true when the secular trend favors inflation and rising inter-est rates. In the business of market forecasting, we can never use the word *guaranteed*, but losing money by holding bonds in a secular inflationary stage 5 environment is about as close as it gets. Some-time in stage 5 or stage 6 defaults start to develop in the high yield bond market, so now is an excellent time to part with these instru-ments before they part with you. There will be an undoubted loss in income as these instruments are rotated into cash, but the increase in safety and longer sleeping hours will more than compensate. One possibility is to purchase high yielding resource-based royalty trusts. They may offer a small capital gain but will more than compensate in yield.

STOCKS

The bulk of equity exposure should now be allocated to late cycle leaders such as resource and basic industry issues. Indeed, the record shows that the most outstanding sector in stage 5 is materials. Occasionally, such as the late 1990s, technology will upstage these other lagging groups, but by and large it is a period when fewer and fewer stocks are on the rise. Do not be fooled if the market averages make new highs because under the surface most stocks are in decline as stage 5 unfolds.

Statistically the market probably rallies more than it declines in stage 5. What is happening is that leading groups (interest-sensitive and other defensive issues) are falling and lagging groups (resource based and basic industry) are rising. If the latter offsets the former, then the averages themselves rise and vice versa. Thus, in the late 1990s the technology sector exploded, and the technology weighting in the S&P 500 increased substantially. As a result, so did the S&P. However, the majority of stocks peaked in 1998, which made it a lot more difficult to make money in 1999 and early 2000 than was suggested by the averages and the technology media hype.

INFLATION HEDGE

Stage 5 is still bullish for commodities and inflation hedge, but this is the last hurrah. The clock has begun to tick, which means that assets should gradually be rotated into cash. This is especially true for commodity bull market highs, where they and their related equities often exhaust themselves in a dramatic peak which shows up in the charts as a price spike, preceded by a parabolic run up. These peaks are difficult to judge unless you have the benefit of hindsight. A gradual liquidation into strength therefore makes sense.

Stage 6 (Nothing Is Bullish)

CASH

At this point cash is definitely king. The cash portion of the portfolio cannot be too high in stage 6. A further advantage of holding liquid cash is that stage 6 is the stage of crises. If something is going to go wrong, this is the time when it is most likely to happen. Stage 1 is another candidate for crises. This also means that it is the time of opportunity, and opportunities often arise when you least expect them. Unfortunately the speed of the decline in some of the markets can be unnerving, which means that the opportunities develop at a time when things look their worst and you feel disinclined to take advantage of them.

BONDS

Bonds are now starting to offer more substantial yields, and it is not usually long after commodity prices start to fall that rates peak out. A *very* gradual entry back into the bond market is therefore possible at some point in stage 6. You have two things working for you. First, the higher rates go, the weaker the economy will be and the greater the bounce in good-quality bond prices during the next bull market. Second, the current return in stage 6 is one of the highest in the cycle, which means that unless you are at the tail end of a secular decline in yields, you will be paid handsomely as you wait for the final bond market low.

Mercifully stage 6, being one of liquidation for all three markets, will typically exist for a very short period, say two to three months or slightly longer. However, a lot of financial damage can be achieved in that short time horizon, so caution is very much the order of the day. We should also say that stage 6 appears to be at its worst when the secular, or very long-term, trend of inflation is rising. Stage 6 environments were far less disruptive between 1981 and 2005 than they were, say, in the 1960s and 1970s.

STOCKS

Bonds generally outperform stocks on a total return basis in stage 6, so there are few reasons for owning any stocks. It is time to think about nibbling away at some of the stage 1 early cycle leaders, but this is generally better done after interest rates peak. Inflation hedge stocks are now usually in a free fall so they should definitely be avoided.

INFLATION HEDGE

Inflation hedge assets try to quickly adjust to this new and bearish stage 6 environment. Because of the leverage associated with the commodity markets, liquidation usually takes place pretty quickly, but there is no reason to jump back in because the bull market in commodities lies three stages into the future.

KEY POINTS

1. Changes in the stages are often realized some time after they have taken place. This is a major justification for making gradual, deliberate asset rotation rather than large quick ones.
2. Larger switches can be justified only when the evidence of a change in the environment is overwhelming and markets have not gone too far in factoring this into the price.
3. The allocations suggested here are general in nature. Actual portfolios should be managed with regard to individual circumstances and the investor's ability and willingness to take on risk, a subject that is taken up elsewhere in this book.
4. Not all cycles will experience all stages. Occasionally, the cycle will skip a stage, and indeed may also retrograde to a previous stage. This is another reason why changes should be gradual.

INDEX

ABOUT THE AUTHORS

Martin J. Pring is regarded as one of the best-known and well-respected figures in financial market analysis. He serves as chief investment strategist at Pring Turner Capital Group.

Joe D. Turner and **Tom J. Kopas** are principals and portfolio managers at Pring Turner Capital Group, a money management firm dedicated to the business cycle investment strategy discussed in *Investing in the Second Lost Decade*. They will comanage the Pring Turner Dow Jones Business Cycle ETF (symbol DBIZ) scheduled for launch by early 2013.